A TRUE BRITISH COLUMBIAN, ALEX MACDONALD SAW the first light of day from the second floor of the Vancouver General Hospital on October 21, 1918. For the two years prior to his birth, his father, M.A. Macdonald, served as B.C.'s Attorney General. When Alex ascended to the same post in 1972, he noted that the office had been out of the family for too long.

Politics and law were to dominate Macdonald's professional life from an early age. He was hired on in Ottawa as secretary to CCF Leader M.J. Coldwell in 1944, thus placing him at the centre of the party's affairs.

He was called to the bar in Ontario in 1947 and in B.C. in 1949. It was in that year that he first aspired to public office and he has been aspiring ever since. Macdonald ran under the CCF banner in British Columbia in 1949 and 1952, losing both times to a right wing coalition aided by the preferential ballot system.

When success finally came it left suddenly. Elected to the House of Commons from Vancouver-Kingsway in 1957, Macdonald soon was deluged by the wave of voters "following John" in 1958. It was back to legal practice for two years.

In 1960, Macdonald was elected MLA for Vancouver East. He has been consistently re-elected since then and is today the "Dean of the Legislature"—B.C.'s longest sitting MLA.

On becoming Attorney General in 1972, Macdonald moved into his father's old office. In a bustle of controversial legal and social reforms, he helped to bring the Justice System into the twentieth century. Concurrently appointed Minister of Industry, he initiated B.C.'s first Development Corporation. As Minister of Energy, he established the B.C. Petroleum Corporation which has since brought $2 billion into the public treasury of the province.

Following the defeat of the NDP government in late 1975, Macdonald resumed the practice of law, paying special attention to his old love by acting as Counsel for trade unions. He continues to sit in the Legislature and is usually found in the eyes of the province's political storms.

'MY DEAR LEGS...'

'MY DEAR LEGS...'

Letters to a
Young Social Democrat

Alex Macdonald

New Star Books
Vancouver, B.C.

First printing July 1985
1 2 3 4 5 89 88 87 86 85

Canadian Cataloguing in Publication Data
Macdonald, Alex, 1918-
'My dear Legs—'

ISBN 0-919573-38-X (bound). —ISBN 0-919573-39-8 (pbk.)

1. Macdonald, Alex, 1918- 2. Politicians - British
Columbia - Biography. 3. New Democratic Party of
British Columbia - Biography. 4. British Columbia -
Politics and government - 1871- I. Title.
FC3828.1.M32A34 1985 971.1'04'0924 C85-091297-0
F1088.M32A34 1985

Typesetting: Stan Persky. Production: Valentina Cambiazo.
Cover design: Klaasen & Beckman. Front cover photo:
Ian McKain. Back cover photo: Hugh Legg.

The publisher is grateful for assistance
provided by the Canada Council.

Printed and bound in Canada by Gagne Printers.

New Star Books Ltd.
2504 York Avenue
Vancouver, B.C.
Canada V6K 1E3

PREFACE

I began writing these letters because the New Democratic Party is losing sight of its cause and may not know where to find it. Putting my Party's troubles into my head, however, soon turned out to be my first mistake. There was scarcely room for them! The pressure made me think, which is a sore treat for any politician. Ah, how much easier it is to make a speech in the Legislature, with my mind on auto pilot while my tongue does the walking.

No matter. Before long I was caught up in a bold attempt not only to unscramble my own brains but also the brains of those John Diefenbaker used to call "my fellow Canadians." Now, all passion spent, I am waiting to hear someone say, "Well, he raised the right questions although some of his answers are questionable." Should a reader fall on something thoroughly annoying in a letter I ask only that it be kindly borne in mind that I was younger when that letter was written. I want mercy not justice. After all, my letters were written with malice toward none (except my Adversaries, who, I hope, will write books that I can pick to pieces).

I have taken care to cleverly hide my preaching among incidents, personalities and even anecdotes. The funny thing is that I am serious. I have retrieved from the past only what seems to me to be relevant and important to our present and future. Briefly, all too briefly, I have recalled

great democratic socialists I have known. Some, like David
Lewis and Frank Scott, no longer with us; others, like
Grace MacInnis, very much alive. Their lives have much to
say to the young of today. More, I think, than anything I
have written, though I have written, or have tried to, in
their footsteps.

These letters have been composed in the autumn of my
political life. I refuse to name the month only because
someone could be hurt in the ensuing scramble for my
nomination. (My friends credit me with every Christian
virtue except resignation.) The letters are age talking to the
coming generation (my doctor told me, "You're fine,
Alex, you'll live to be 65," knowing full well that I was
66). They are addressed to Hugh Legg, widely known as
"Legs," a callow youth now half my age and rapidly
catching up. By now only a single generation separates us,
as his daughter plays with my grandchildren. Yes, Legs
really lives, and scampers with me on the squash court
every week or so. He joined the NDP in 1975 for what he
says were religious reasons. He was quite beside himself
when the Pope landed at Flatrock, Newfoundland, last
year and confirmed that the needs of the poor must come
before the desires of the rich. He hit the ball so hard that
he beat me, something I hold to be a rare occasion. Legs'
father is a Judge and judges run in the family: my father,
and now both my big and little brother. I'd have made an
excellent judge myself, only my attention span is too long.
Instead I fell among Legislators. My father, then Chief
Justice of British Columbia, used to be riled to read in the
Elections Act that the only persons who could not sit in the
Legislature were "Judges, Indians and Lunatics." Since
then an Indian has been seated, no judges of course, and
quite a few lunatics, whom I readily recognize. So will the
reader who perseveres.

Of course there is criticism in these letters but I have
tried to make it friendly and positive. In our anxious times

too many, especially interest groups, equate any criticism with mortal enmity. They should be like me and welcome criticism (in tiny, measured dollops!). Continuous, trenchant public examination of institutions and policies is the only avenue to progressive change. "If Way to the Better there be, it exacts a full Look at the Worst."

And, yes, come to think of it, I have even criticized my own Party. What! Criticize a Party that would have me for a member? Why not? And why not openly? Political parties are public institutions and should wash their clothes at the creek with other folk. Otherwise they inspire distrust. I speak out because I believe the NDP must take new directions. The unions, its partner in a socialist future, must also transform their present negative power into the positive power of self-discipline and decision-making.

The letters say that Canadians are living beyond their means. (I can spot that as I have been living beyond my own intellectual means for years.) Not all Canadians. Many, far too many, have too slender means; many have means too fat. In the aggregate, however, our expectations and consumptions are running ahead of our production of marketable goods and services. There are many symptoms —an eroding industrial base, a national debt rising to the trigger point of a new chemistry when money is borrowed to pay interest on money owing. Public debt, socialists please note, will be a headache for any Progressive Government and supports the arguments of the enemies of social programs. It is ironic, but nonetheless true, that at a time when science has made abundance for all a perfectly practicable matter it cannot be achieved without putting checks upon inordinate self-seeking.

The letters also speak of a breakdown in values. Yesterday's ill-gotten gains become today's ancestral fortunes. Money neither cares nor knows to whom it flows. "Slow rises worth by poverty oppressed," and merit is a depreciated coin in the market place. Everyone has choices but some, unfairly, have far more choices than others. Opportunities, as well as wealth, must be redistributed.

I hope the letters reflect flashes of anger. They still visit me almost as keenly as in the days of my youth. In 1942, when I was a Secretary to M.J. Coldwell, the CCF Leader, I abused my editorial position by inserting a little article of my own in the CCF *News*. I was outraged by the exploitation and premature deaths of the tin miners of Bolivia while the Patino family, who owned the mines and ran the government and the police of Bolivia, were living it up in luxury and sin in Paris. I finished my article off with the lines, "The people, Lord, the people; not Kings and Crowns but men." Ah, was I giving off more heat than light? No doubt about it.

Even today some will espy a well of emotion at the bottom of my beliefs. I have no apologies for that. The heart has its logic as the head has its, and the first is harder to acquire than the second. And even the head, abetted by the heart, can only search endlessly for certain truth. We score a goal and the goal posts recede and we must score again. What matters is never to abandon the search and to insist upon righting rightable wrongs.

My thanks are due to my editor, Lanny Beckman, who removed the sin from my syntax and even inserted a sense of humus in passages that had nothing to do with agriculture. Thanks also to Janet Duckworth, who debated points with me to telling effect. Also to Legs for lobbing questions at me and refusing to take a simple yes or no for an answer. And thanks, finally, to the loyal voters who have given me their ballots even though many came to know me better than I know myself!

This collection is dedicated to my wife, Dorothy, whom I married at an early urge and who has brought me up through rough passages into my peaceful years of indiscretion.

Alex Macdonald
The Legislature
Victoria, B.C.
March 27, 1985

'MY DEAR LEGS...'

'WHERE LIES THE LAND
TO WHICH THE SHIP WOULD GO?'

The Legislature
Victoria, B.C.
August 29, 1983

My dear Legs,

Last evening when the Legislature adjourned, some of our MLAs came to my office to hear the returns from the federal by-election in Mission-Port Moody. I produced a bottle of scotch from my filing cabinet, just in case. Sure enough, the scotch disappeared. Our so-called safe seat fell to Brian Mulroney. Shoals of Liberal voters skooted toward his Pretty Face, passing right over our candidate.

The NDP should be doing fine with the economy wallowing in recession. But it's not. And it didn't in the provincial election last May when the floating voters held their noses and scratched "X"s for Bill Bennett. They wouldn't take a chance on us. What is it we are not doing right?

One MLA volunteered that we'll do better when the economy gets—not worse—but better! If so, a fat lot those floating voters think of our economic program.

Ah, Legs, we have come a long way from the CCF movement to the NDP Party—too far, if you ask me. The early CCFers reckoned that if they stood fast for what was right people would come their way, sooner or later. Yet if they were too idealistic, the NDP is the opposite—too opportunistic. Sometimes I think the NDP is beginning to quack, waddle and gabble like any other party for whom winning elections is the goal. That's all very well for, say, the Oldline Parties whose goals are to get into office, get the trough jobs and stay put. But the NDP needs a different reason for existence. Besides, even if winning elections was all that mattered, there's just no political space in Canada for another party like the others.

You know what those floating voters say about us behind our backs? That NDPers get their economics from the Canadian Labour Congress, that we don't care about efficiency on the job or rewards based on merit. And they put us down as a give-away bunch—every outstretched hand will be filled—so used to saying "yes" that we are downright promiscuous. They think of socialism as the time when

> *the Brave New World begins,*
> *Where all men are paid for existing*
> *And no man pays for his sins.*

Sure, they are laying a bum rap on us, but that's how we have made them see us. Dammit, Legs, socialism is a *more* disciplined society, one that says, Stop, think of the needs of others, think of the safety and the health of the Whole State of which you are a part.

Oh, we have an image problem all right—deeper than just not having the advertising bucks—compounded when we forget what we are really all about.

We need time out to think things over, to rediscover our compass bearings and set course for the future. If we are off course now, as I think we are, we better know why, and where we took the wrong turns. Not that I'm any pilot. I'm as responsible for poor directions as any other NDPers. I've played the elections games, told people what they want to hear and promised more goodies than there were to go round. Criticizing my own party doesn't come easily. I feel as if I am kicking my own dog. I joined the CCF 40 years ago. Forty years! As long as the Israelites wandered in the Wilderness! Long enough, perhaps, to give me a licence to murmur a little—even an obligation.

So today I am at my desk in the Legislature scribbling to you. Me, Yesterday's Man, talking to you, little more than a runny nose kid. At least there's relief in it from the boredom that has fallen on this Chamber like August heat. Our MLAs have been filibustering all of Bennett's legislation, not just the restraint Bills, since last June. Right now, a couple of desks away, an NDPer is in the middle of a long speech against the lifting of rent controls—which I made law in 1973. So he should be—rich landlords will get more money from poor tenants. But, my God, these speeches go on and on.

This dreary Session is trying to tell me some of what's wrong with us. Strong on tactics. Weak on alternatives. Bennett, who was as surprised at winning the election last May as we were at losing it, lost no time calling the Legislature and bringing down his ham-fisted restraint budget. And, with the budget, all at once, 31 Bills; freezing wages, wiping out the Human Rights Commission, putting services to disadvantaged children out to tender, and so on. All his gamey bottom-line fantasies.

Our Caucus decided to block all 31 Bills. Many of them did deserve a long, rough ride but others were run-of-the-mill Bills we really agreed with. So through the slow summer we've had slower speeches as Legislative democracy was jammed. Now in the dog days of August I'm getting visions of well-marshalled filibustering going on for months. Forces of accomplished bores, including myself, in groups of seven (the others resting) taking the floor until everyone's patience is worn out. I'm scared people will find us out! This place is like a sieve. Even the media let things out and gremlins do the rest, carrying the word to the folks back home.

Perhaps my irascibility says more about me than our Parliamentary tactics, but I don't think so. Tedium sweeps the real issues out of sight. I believe socialists have to make Parliaments respected, Legs, even if they have to become respectable to do it. For they have no other way to make social change while preserving basic liberties. I like the clash of to-the-point debate on things that matter. And I'm for the NDP giving clear alternatives and owning up to unpleasant realities. Some say that even though Mulroney's Conservatives in opposition won't say what they'd do, they are going to win anyway. More like *because* they won't say. But if we were like that I wouldn't have joined 40 years ago.

Oh, oh. Robin Blencoe has just called the Minister of Labour a fool. Mr. Speaker rouses himself. But another of our MLAs quickly intervenes with the observation that no one should be allowed to call that Honourable Minister a fool—that would be revealing government secrets. Blencoe withdraws his slur; Mr. Speaker subsides.

Our tactics would be better if we really knew who we are and where we want to go. Roy Hattersley recalls how he and Tony Crosland played a game on the weekend before Tony died—how to define socialism in one sentence. Both had served as Cabinet Ministers in the Labour governments in Britain. Crosland dealt up: "Socialism is about the pursuit of equality, the protection of liberty and the understanding that until we are all equal we shall not be free." He didn't mean absolute equality of incomes. The bad old world isn't ready for that. Nor were his ideas all that original. Herodotus, the Father of History, was on the same track 2,500 years earlier when he wrote, "Freedom and Equality are fine spirit-stirring things." That's the heart of the matter for socialists, yesterday and tomorrow. Programs are simply the means we devise to achieve those ends.

Last night I dined on a fine chicken in Victoria's exclusive Union Club. MLAs can sign chits there, inconspicuous among the still living. My waitress told me that she gets twenty hours of work at the minimum wage as a salesgirl, and some hours on call at the Union Club. She's in her late twenties, chipper and peppy. Has a car, she says, but doesn't drive it much because of the cost of gasoline. Rides a bike instead, and asks me if it's still windy outside. I say the wind will die down when the Legislature rises. Then I'm off, surmising, my bleeding heart pumping away. She'll not land a 9 to 5 husband, or even an 8 to 4 one; never make a killing on the stock exchange; never have a home of her own. She'll get by, in relative deprivation, increasingly aware of the showy extravagances around her and the conspicuous wastes. Will her self-esteem slowly seep away in self-reproach?

Societies should be judged by their treatment of their most vulnerable citizens. Ill-treatment of the least diminishes everyone. All the Great Teachers of Mankind have done their best to drive this point home.

The inequalities seemed more out in the open for everyone to see and care about when I was attracted by socialism in the thirties. Hungry men rode box cars looking for work or did road work in the relief camps for 25 cents a day. Now the inequalities that mark the actual living experiences of individuals are glossed over as if they didn't matter much. Who's to care, when there is welfare for those down and out, when unemployment is only a seasonally adjusted statistic that rolls around once a month, and when TV ads boil over with vast stores of useful and useless wealth? The working poor? Well, they could do better if they only tried harder, or so say the self-appointed Lords of the Organs of Public Opinion.

I fell for the CCF in 1943 because of its principles—not its election programs. Even the ringing declaration at the end of the Regina Manifesto, that "no CCF government will rest content until capitalism is eradicated," was fine with me. The excitement comes back when I take from my drawer a Charter issued to the Cedar Cottage CCF Club in 1938. On the yellowing parchment are inscribed the words, "The CCF is a Federal organization whose purpose is the establishment in Canada of a Co-operative Commonwealth in which the principle regulating production, distribution and exchange will be the supplying of needs and not the making of profit."

I'm still for that. My principles are not dated. Just me. My wife has become the youngest person in Canada receiving the Old Age Pension. She grabs my cheques off the postman. Conditions change; new remedies are needed, not new principles. The CCF was more up front about where it wanted to go than the NDP is today. CCFers didn't keep their purposes in a hip pocket like a flask of whiskey to have a pull on when no one was watching.

So in 1943 I climbed wooden stairs to a cluttered little office on Sparks Street in Ottawa. There David Lewis, the CCF National Secretary, rummaged around on his desk and found a membership blank. I signed it. Thereby Canada lost in me a future, capital Pfogg-bound Senator. But David softened the blow by offering me a salary cut to go to work on Parliament Hill for CCF Leader M.J. Coldwell, as his whatever. I jumped at it.

Soon I was on the job in M.J.'s office, Room 626, at a small table squeezed in behind the door. When M.J. was away, however, I became the presence behind his desk, looking like the kid on the cover of Mad Magazine, with freckles, jug ears and an earnest, toothy grin. I still drop in to Room 626, now the anteroom to Ed Broadbent's office, with an eerie feeling of time standing still. The NDP is no stronger today in a somewhat larger House of Commons than the CCF was after the 1945 election.

Coldwell had left Colchester, England, for the endless prairies and became a teacher. School out, he used to sally forth on the rutted or muddy roads to preach socialism in drafty country halls, billet overnight and get back to school with the rising sun. In 1935 the farmers of Rosetown-Biggar made him their Member of Parliament.

Rosetown reminds me of a trip I made with M.J. to his constituency. In a gathering of farmers I asked, "What's the stubble used for?" The farmers held their sides, rocking with laughter. I still don't know.

When M.J. rose in the Commons he was a courtly figure, his glasses now and then propped on his nose. He spoke with a trace of English accent, sometimes indignantly but never sullenly, and everyone listened with respect. What was there to fear in a Leader whose habits allowed, after services at St. Mark's Anglican Church, as a special Sunday treat, a single bottle of beer? With clarity and grace he expressed the CCF objective. "What we seek," he said, "is a society which would include opportunities for worthwhile service, with adequate rewards for work well done." His emphasis was on service to others. "Something for Nothing" was not dreamt of in his philosophy, as it is not dreamt of in many of the great guiding systems of thought. Capitalism is an obvious exception here, which perhaps explains its obsession with spurning the principle it so cherishes. M.J.'s appeal was to the inner pride everyone has in contributing to the common good; paying back, with interest, what society gives.

In the war years, support for the CCF surged until the wave crested and broke in 1945. People were saying "never again" to the Hungry Thirties and the war. Farm boys became militant unionists in the factories; a planned economy spewed out plenty for the troops and the home front. If for war, why not for peace? If for guns and canteens, why not for homes and hamburgers?

Where to draw the line, Legs, between the tactics that win elections and the fight for principles that represent basic social change? During the war years the CCF began a slow descent into the realm of nitty-gritty political stickhandling. Already in 1944 the watering down of the Regina Manifesto had begun. I sat in a hall in the Windsor Hotel in Montreal where David Lewis led the debate for a more moderate statement of principles. Still, what remained was pretty spunky stuff—socialization of the banks and financial institutions and industries "monopolistic in character." Small businesses would be private, however, if they served a useful purpose.

Spunky enough to scare the fat cats of privilege out of their boots. While their Old Parties exchanged polite debating points with the CCF MPs in Parliament their power brokers in the country released the sewer rats of fear and loathing. Their ad agencies put propaganda into every home insisting that a CCF victory would bring the tyranny of jackbooted National Socialism (their code words for Naziism), where anyone's name could turn up on a secret list of those who were to be "looked after." If the CCF was spared, for a time, from comparisons to Godless Communism it was only because everyone's kindly uncle, the pipe-smoking Man of Steel, Joseph Stalin, was then our gallant ally.

And the Old Parties made quick left-turns. The CCF was force marching them toward the Welfare State. They decked themselves out as ardent social reformers, in the process stealing some of the CCF's clothes—family allowances and unemployment insurance among them. The lesson for us, Legs, is to have enough policies in our wardrobe so as not to go naked when some are stolen.

The CCF wave crested in the late war years before breaking in 1945. It swept Saskatchewan in 1944. In B.C., however, Liberals and Conservatives held onto power by forming a coalition. In Ontario, after almost winning in 1943, the CCF was repulsed in a fierce counterattack. Still I think it's best to keep our principles out front as the CCF did in those years. There will be flak but if we patiently respond, each succeeding volley they fire at us will be less effective.

Tommy Douglas struck the right balance between political expediency and socialist goals. In the spring of 1944 he was down the hall from M.J.'s office in shirt sleeves packing his papers into cardboard boxes. He had resigned his seat to fight the Saskatchewan election as CCF Provincial Leader. On a small card he had drawn up ten points, ready for the printers, as his program for a first term in office. He was in earnest about each of the ten points—no more, no less—promises made were debts to be paid.

Tommy was a more political cat than M.J. I sat on the platform of the Regina High School for one of his speeches. When his five-foot-and-some figure rose to speak, a wag shouted, "Stand up Tommy." He joined in the laughter. His speech began with humorous stories until he and his audience were afloat together. Then the message, without a hint of inner doubt, simple and direct, followed by the peroration with its vision of a New Jerusalem. No one fidgeted although the speech was long, and Tommy allowed afterwards that he "had passed some good stopping points." All his speeches seemed to flow spontaneously, but in fact had been carefully crafted.

Tommy Douglas did not run for office to mind the store better than his opponents, or to slap on a new coat of paint. All his election programs were part of taking down the store and putting up a new one; not all at once, but for sure.

Douglas extended public ownership during his terms in office, beginning with the socialization of auto and fire insurance. Alas, in these degenerate days, public ownership is no longer fashionable in the best NDP circles; not something to be mentioned in public anyway. What! Has the Radical Right got our tongue? Please explain to me, Legs, why, if share ownership is a good thing, everyone owning the shares isn't a better thing. Or is such equality, in the words of Marie Antoinette (after sharing *herself*), "much too good for the common people"?

In 1944 geologists brought Premier Douglas reports of rich potash reserves in southern Saskatchewan. Tommy's imagination was fired by prospects of revenues at home and fertilizers abroad to revitalize the tired soils of a hungry world. Unhappily his treasury was bare. So he asked Ottawa to participate with Saskatchewan in joint public development. No, sniffed Ottawa, too socialistic. Next he sought British participation through his friend Sir Stafford Cripps, who was Chancellor of the Exchequer in the Labour Government. Now Ottawa decreed that the niceties of diplomatic protocol did not permit the province to negotiate with a foreign state. Reluctantly Tommy dispatched his Minister of Finance, Clarence Fines, to sell the potash rights on the money markets of New York. Practical realities made him buy time.

By 1975 multinational companies looked on the potash of Saskatchewan as their very own. They sent packing the provincial inspectors who came to look at the books. They hired a force of lawyers to argue that the province which licensed their business had no right to draw royalties from what had become an international trade. They refused to modernize their plants or increase production when scarcities brought them higher prices and profits.

In November, 1975, Premier Alan Blakeney, in Tommy's old office, had secret plans to socialize half the potash industry ready to go. As a courtesy he sent word of the coming announcement to Premier Dave Barrett in Victoria. Dave summoned me downstairs to his office. He was coatless as usual, stocking feet pacing the carpet, worried that headlines about takeovers in Saskatchewan would give our Socred foes ammunition in the B.C. election set for December. He called Blakeney, asking him to postpone his announcement but Blakeney replied that his well-timed plans were too advanced to be put off. Blakeney weathered his storm and was re-elected. He had restored to the people of Saskatchewan resources that should have been theirs all along. This was not, I hope, Legs, the last Socialistic Hurrah of the old CCFers.

The NDP has to sell public ownership of resources and large enterprises on practical grounds, well-researched, case by case, as well as by ideology.

The Right invites everyone to Beware of Big Government, and I invite you, Legs, to Beware of the Big Business Establishment. Frankly, I don't notice governments pushing big business around; quite the opposite as a matter of fact. The democratic state, large, sprawling, beset by powerful interest groups, unable to command events, is above all weak; big business isn't.

No one wants too much power heaped up in one pile, either in a state or anywhere else. And yet the dispersal of power can only be brought about through democratic choice, exercised at all levels of government. The Crown Corporation would form an economic centrepiece of a sane society, jointly run by management and workers, autonomous in most business decisions, competing with their counterparts so they stay honest and efficient, and, overall, responsive to the public interest.

My daughter used to be a bus checker for public B.C. Hydro before she began to present me with semi-Dutch grandchildren. The checkers stood on street corners and timed the arrival of buses, their passenger loads and so on. An electronic eye could do that cheaper, but what really is cheaper if the checkers join the ranks of the unemployed? I want social considerations to be part of that kind of decision-making.

Private corporations, even on good behaviour, are committed to the profit expectations of their shareholders, which obliges them to be as efficient as possible, with slight if any regard paid to social considerations. I simply want to change their priorities; make the corporate giants primarily concerned with important public interests, and secondarily cost-effective and efficient. (Don't believe them when they protest that those two things go hand in hand. That's called—I'll put it politely—propaganda.)

Without economic democracy Canada will continue to have her privileged elites; without political democracy Russia will continue to have hers.

When too much socialism is dropped from our day to day talking the Party loses oomph. In the provincial election last May I went around to church halls and schools to debate my Social Credit opponents. They brought with them a noisy claque of young far-right Reaganites who never let up on me. They were True Believers and all fired up. Downsize government! Cut services! Let 'em fend for themselves! I told them they were tearing up whole Chapters of the New Testament. They hardly heard me. Socialism was an old discarded dogma ready for the ashcan of history. I believe otherwise but these young people were as numerous and zealous for their philosophy as our young people are for ours. That I didn't like.

Why preach at you! I'm the one who needs a good talking to. Nevertheless, you'll hear more. This Session has a way to go. Our Caucus is friendly in spite of disagreements. Still, what a Session! Historically, Canadian Legislatures wind up their Sessions when the bores begin to bore the bores. But the delights of ennui are not for me. I prefer girls.

"Where lies the Land to which the Ship would go?"
Legs, the sailors *must* know.

Admonitorily yours,

Alex

TO THOSE WHO HAVE SHALL BE GIVEN

The Legislature
Victoria, B.C.
September 6, 1983

Dear Legs,

I should have listened to my speech—it was quite good, or so I'm told, Mr. Speaker nodding away through the whole thing. I spoke against Bennett's restraint program, must have, we all do. The funny thing is that I too am for restraint, though not his kind. I want to see restraints on the income of those who get too much, in order to be able to bring up the incomes of those who get too little.

For a year now Bennett has been heavily into his kind of restraint (no, I don't mean Stocks and Bonds!). His kind counts on reducing or doing away with government departments and agencies, cutting back public services and curbing the wages of public employees. His heart bleeds, and did all through the last election, for someone he calls *the taxpayer*, conveniently forgetting that there are well-heeled taxpayers who have more than enough left over, and taxpayers with holes in the heels of their socks with nothing left over. Bennett is also one of too many today who think that one good way to provide housing for the poor is to build tax shelters for the rich. He also thinks, though you won't catch him saying it publicly, that a pool of unemployment makes people work harder and accept lower wages for fear of falling in. And, above all, he believes that everyone is a lot better off when some make a lot more than others. How do we answer the trumpery of a man like that, Legs? With arguments that are deeper than his are shallow, that's how. So follow me as I explain how extensive and inhumane inequalities are today, and show how they cannot be justified by any good they are doing to the economy and how they can be narrowed. Later I'll go into medical care as an example of a service that provides many exorbitant professional incomes, we being none the healthier for the inequities, and I'll also point out that evening out incomes must usually be accompanied by pretty basic reforms in the services or industries involved.

Of course, you don't need deep arguments to convince a banquet of NDPers and trade unionists that Bennett's make-the-rich-richer stuff is not for them. So last Saturday, I had a fine old time stamping on Bennett's kind of restraint at the annual salmon barbecue of the Delta NDP. No, Legs, my speech was not as nourishing as the salmon, but hear this, I got a standing ovation, although that was a bit of a fluke. Art Kube, President of the B.C. Federation of Labour, spoke first. When he finished his stemwinder one of his men at a front table stood up clapping hard, first bringing that table to its feet, and, by semaphore, two other tables of his supporters who were positioned at the back corners of the hall. Soon the whole gathering was on its feet, applauding. So when I finished I gave a quick, sharp look at his man at the front table, who started to his feet, bringing up, etc., etc., until the whole crowd was up again applauding my speech, including those helping as cooks, who came out of the kitchen to see what was going on.

However, suppose I had got into deeper answers and, in addition to bashing Bennett's restraint, had gone on to talk about the other incomes that will have to be restrained if we are serious about social equality. What would the cooks have thought about that? NDPers are used to their MLAs attacking bank profits and sundry other rip-offs of the corporate elite. They are not used to hearing them even suggest that limits may have to be placed on the levels of salaries and professional fees and, certainly, not on wages. Perhaps I should have given them that surprise, but I didn't and sat down to enjoy my standing ovation.

Half a century has passed since the CCF proclaimed in the Regina Manifesto that "the present order is marked by glaring inequalities in wealth and opportunity." Ah, we think, those bad old Depression days! In fact, 50 years later, those inequalities are more glaring than ever; yes, in spite of our vaunted Welfare State, with family allowances and other services, and a graduated income tax, the inequalities have deepened. If our principal goal, Legs, is fair returns for all, as it is, we are losing the war. And while we have been losing the war because we just didn't get enough votes we are also losing it in another way, when the NDP becomes content with simply advancing and defending the Welfare State. The Regina Manifesto didn't say that social services and a fair tax system would be enough in themselves to eliminate the inequalities. These were to be only some of the economic tools required to bring about fair sharing and to give everyone a chance to work.

How badly we are losing the war can be seen not only by looking around and meeting people, but in the statistics as well. The statistics tell us that in 1951 the top 20 per cent of those receiving incomes were getting seven times as much as the bottom 20 per cent; by 1976 the top 20 per cent were getting fifteen times as much as the bottom 20 per cent. Later figures will show that this trend toward a widening of the gap between the well-off and the poor is continuing. Moreover, among the 60 per cent between the tops and bottoms, there are also widening inequalities in wealth and opportunity. There are, for example, dishwashers who make about a fifth of a decent union wage in a secure business. That gap is too wide and it is simplistic to think that we can ratchet up the lower wages while letting the market system, with all its pressure groups that now determine wage levels, go on as before.

Of course, the statistics also tell us that average per capita wealth has increased substantially over the years and that infant mortality is down and life expectancy is up. It is true that those on social assistance have "more" than many did in earlier years, but we have to remember that poverty lies in the lack of those things reasonably regarded as necessary for a decent life in any particular age or society. Farther back, in the times of Robbie Burns, the farmers of Ayreshire had little enough of those material things now regarded as necessities of life. What rankled with Robbie, however, as it should with us, was the way what little they had was parcelled out:

> *It's hardly in a bodies power,*
> *To keep at times from being sour*
> *To see how things are shared*

Take the case of a young man who was fired by one of the grain terminal companies and suddenly began to share in much less of the good things of life. He was referred to me by the union, to size up his chances of reinstatement under the grievance procedure. Unfortunately, he had made more than one stupid mistake and the firing had to stand. This was a severe sentence. At the terminal he had been making $14.81 per hour along with fringe benefits that included a medical and dental plan, a retirement pension, sickness wage indemnity, and life insurance. Now he is driving a cab at night for about $400 per month, making less in a month than he earned in a week as a grainworker with none of those social benefits.

I think of the Superintendent of Schools for Vancouver,

a good one, who has a salary of $89,000 a year. This is higher than the Premier's and slightly lower than that of the Chief Justice of Canada. In the same city a retired nurse lives in a dingy walk-up flat on a pension income of $7,000 a year, with a black and white television, often on the blink, and a dog whose diet is almost as rich as hers. When the Superintendent's salary came up, a friend of mine says, yes, it's high, but comparable to what's paid in other provinces. And, she added, the amount hardly matters among the millions spent on education. I can't help thinking it matters quite a lot. My thrifty Scottish bones murmur that three families, supported by three jobs, could live well on a third each of that salary. And that there are numberless other big and bigger salaries, public and private, that could spread themselves and let some others live a little easier.

Why is there such a discrepancy between what the Superintendent makes and what the nurse receives? Well, the Superintendent is at the apex of a large educational establishment. Its members play a very natural game of catch-up, and the more the Superintendent earns the more a principal can aspire to, and the administrators, and so on down the line. Some educators say that a School Board has to pay this kind of money to get a qualified Super-intendent. Some even suggest, and this is nonsense, that the man wouldn't work as well if he were paid less. Ah, Legs, it is part of the folklore of capitalism to suggest that the qualified men behind the big desks must be paid like kings; and a very convenient part it is to those who do well. It is even convenient to lawyers who like their clients to believe the myth that the more they pay the lawyer the better off they will be before the old Judge. Such myths, Legs, ought to be detonated. What! Would a Judge administer the law less well if he were paid less, or hand out shorter sentences? Possibly today he would, tomorrow he mustn't.

The "distance" between the Superintendent's income (plus retirement pension) and the nurse's income, and between what the young grainworker earned before and after he was fired, is unconscionably far. In another letter I'll collect my thoughts (that won't take long; unlawful assembly some will call it) and show how these distances can be shortened by a fair incomes policy.

Am I exaggerating the extent of the unfairness, Legs? I bet that's what you are thinking. Part of me thinks so. The other day in a Safeway in the East End, pushing a cart, I exchanged hellos with pensioners and just plain working folk. There were more smiling faces than despondent ones. They seemed to carry on as if the social injustices I am railing about either didn't exist or weren't hurting many. Hurt many they do. Still I have uneasy feelings bringing up the Superintendent's salary. He does render good public service. Someday there'll be so much that it won't matter if we splurge on some. Not now. Meanwhile, let's not neglect the old familiar targets, the ill-gotten gains, for instance, of the parasitic traders who buy and sell discounted second mortgages or those who make money selling short the Canadian dollar, or the banks, or the oil companies. No, I haven't forgotten my old adversaries! Who owns that Safeway I was in, Legs? There is no safe-way! A dwindling few conglomerates are taking over our food outlets. They're not in business to produce food but to make money. Read Jack Warnock's *Profit Hungry*. They amass profits in New York and Chicago. They merge and takeover one another, and trade the same Directors around as if they were spouses at a swap party. With cut prices, give-away samples, zebra stripes, and billions advertising differences that don't exist, they drive little competitors out of the market and manage prices to suit themselves. Tinted Lemonades! Bird's Eye broccoli in synthetic sauce and plastic wrap! Pretty soon we'll need a Degree in Chemistry to eat.

If only the profits of the corporations (after clipping off the coupon-clipper) could stretch far enough to cover the needs of social programs, adequate incomes for all, plant modernization and the capital needs of secondary industries. They won't stretch that far.

Yes, industrial growth. I'm not just a spread the wealth man, Legs, though you may have that impression. The economy is not like a poker game where whatever anyone around the table wins, someone else loses. Adding to the common store is at least as important as how it is dealt out.

And, to show you how fair I am, Legs, I enter, as an Exhibit for the Defence, Ian Sinclair of the CPR, who gave back more for what he took out than any other tycoon I can think of. He had the largest take-home pay of anyone I have run into (I don't get around all that much). Tycoons' salaries are hush-hush in Canada but you can look them up in Washington, D.C. In one recent year, Sinclair's salaries included $271,484 from C.P. Ltd. and $228,344 from C.P. Enterprises Ltd. Now poor Ian has gone to his reward, stretching his weary limbs at last on a bed of patronage in the Canadian Senate.

I met Sinclair in Premier Dave Barrett's office in Victoria back in 1973. After a while he brought up our plan to raise the minimum wage from $1.75 to $2.50 an hour. This, he protested, would put the CPR's Empress Hotel in the red. Dave flew into orbit, defying Sinclair to go on TV and say that the CPR couldn't afford to pay chambermaids $2.50, and declaring he'd go on too with a pledge to take back all the acres the CPR had got for nothing. When silence fell, acting as Interpreter, and twiddling my soggy cigar butt, I observed, "What the Premier means, Mr. Sinclair, is that the minimum wage is going to $2.50."

I last saw Ian on a C.P. plane to Montreal as he swept up the aisle past my tourist seat and stopped for some pleasantries. Before his shiny pants disappeared behind the first-class curtain he lifted a cigar from my jacket pocket, claiming he had forgotten his. I expected he'd send back a postprandial brandy but no such luck. Thrift is among his Canadian virtues.

I'm not complaining about the size of Sinclair's salaries just to be disliked by a better class of person. I just want them spread out to make several productive jobs. Others argue that big rewards to some result in more investment in the economy. But in a properly planned economy, in which individuals were fairly compensated, almost everyone, one way or another, would participate in capital formation.

It's a long way down from Sinclair to the kids hanging out on Granville Mall, a guitar case beseeching change, drop-outs from the peer pressures in school, beyond hope of a job. Robert Louis Stevenson wrote that "to travel hopefully is better than to arrive." These kids travel without hope. Unlike Sinclair, their get-up and go has got up and gone. I trust not forever, but I am far from sure.

What makes people apply themselves, become able to make their own opportunities? Socialists have thought too little of this. We know what destroys incentive—prolonged idleness in early life destroys it. Lack of youth employment opportunities is a costly social crime, one likely to be with us for years unless things change.

Some kinds of get-up and go we can do without. There is, for example, a local millionaire who's behind the cash register seven days a week except for time at his fundamentalist church where he takes short respites from the worship of Mammon. The story goes that when he put together his first sales dealership he fired the salesman with the lowest sales each month. I guess that would promote hustle. It reminds me of the French Foreign Legion where they'd shoot the odd Legionnaire "pour encourager les autres."

We need several kinds of incentive, based on more than

just hustling for a buck. Inventors invent for money but even more for the satisfaction of discovery. My friend Knute Boelt, who imports dairy products, told me about the Danish farmer who invented a better churn that got twelve pounds of feta cheese instead of ten from 100 pounds of milk. What moved him to a method that increased productivity to the benefit of his country? Money, a creative incentive, but moreso, I would say, the pleasure of having others say, "well done." Few young people fortunate enough to enter the job market today, however, will have that farmer's chance. Most of the work in Canada is so mechanized and organized from the top down that workers are met with a "Keep Out" sign on the door to the Creative Department.

I confess the question of what moves people to give their best seemed easy to me years ago. Of course they wanted to help others as much as themselves! I basked in poetry:

As they laid him back in the earth
Remembering the straining Red Flags
They record simply
How this one excelled all others in
Making driving belts.

By now I've learned that even in a decent social order there will have to be cash bonuses for extra effort, even some catering to the human vanity of making more than someone else. Yet, through the years I've run into damn few who didn't want the self-fulfilment of being useful.

And so, moving right along, I'm into health care, which touches everyone, and provides examples of big income peaks while making my extra point that smoothing them out will by no means solve all of the problems in the system. Most of the income peaks go to the doctors or to dentists, to some of them much more than to others. Many doctors I speak with are as concerned as I am about the inequities, although they do not share my opinion that they flow from the fee-for-service method of payments. I am saying, Legs, that doctors and dentists would perform as well for less money, which I insist is a compliment although they may not take it as such.

You needn't worry. The irrevocable catastrophe which the medical profession does more than hint at simply won't materialize.

No, your libido wouldn't last longer if your doctor made more money! No, the quality of medical care would not deteriorate if many doctors didn't make seven times as much money as their patients. Ah, but would levelling out doctors' incomes free up enough dollars to make a significant difference to others? The answer is "yes," for there are lots of dollars involved, and if you will listen a while, I'll give you hard numbers from the medical plan.

First let me give you a surgeon, a fine one no doubt, who is on the golf links every afternoon and who, according to the government's book, drew a gross of $274,036 from the plan in 1983. Taking off the salary of his reception-ist/nurse and the expenses of a small office (not the hospital overhead; the public purse pays that) still leaves him, along with most medical specialists, on the top rungs of the ladder of inequality. Coming down the ladder (being careful when passing the P.M.), you find a skilled technician who works in a bio-medical laboratory for $26,000 a year. On a lower rung you find an actor making $6,000 to bring live theatre to the parched natives in the Canadian wasteland. Also clinging to this low rung is a single mother getting $6,000 a year, out of which she has to pay 40 per cent as rent for a run-down flat, while also feeding and clothing two children. I have left out still higher and lower rungs and simply remind you that the ladder of inequality does stretch further in both directions.

Now let's have a look at Dr. William Jory. A study of his case may reward us with some answers to my various questions. Dr. Jory is an ophthalmologist who was elected President of the B.C. Medical Association in 1982. He languishes for part of the year as a landed gentleman in Hampshire, England, with ritzy neighbours. The rest of the year he ministers to eyes in these parts (sometimes from his tax-deductible yacht, the Aeolus, named for the Greek God of Wind). In 1982 he received $232,776 from our medical plan. I trust he shares some of it with his wife for her services as his assistant.

Our Skeena MP, Jim Fulton, had the audacity to say that Dr. Jory examined the eyes of 114 northern Native Indians at Port Simpson in 71 minutes. If Fulton were right, and assuming each of the Indians had two eyes, that works out to one eye looked into every nineteen seconds, with no one falling down. Dr. Jory had more eye-contact in two days than Don Juan had in a lifetime—and received payment in coin of the realm, $5,700 for his two-day yacht-stop at Port Simpson.

In a spirited defence, Dr. Jory replied, "An examination doesn't take that long for gosh sakes." And later (forgetting that many northern denizens are quite bereft of medical or dental care), he observed that the Medical Association should limit the influx of new doctors by using "a filter with smaller holes."

Still, Fulton's charges obliged the Medical College to lay five counts of "infamous conduct" against the famous Dr. Jory. The hearing before his peers slowly unwinds, behind closed doors. The public will not have a look-see at the evidence of how their money is spent. When plain citizens are tried on matters of less public moment, the sun shines in; the goings-on of this elite are shrouded in darkness. Only the Jory verdict will be known, and I suspect the College will have to nail the good doctor on one count or other. The doctors who sit in judgment, however, will not be so indelicate as to question the size of his income (or their own)—only his slipshod ways. I, however, must question sizes for the connection between physician affluence and the relative poverty of many of the patients is short and direct. The patients pay premiums and taxes that pass quickly through the plan to the physicians; usually dollars follow a more circuitous route from poverty to private affluence.

The number of dollars passing through our plan has been rising exponentially in recent years. In 1978-79, the fee-for-service payouts from the plan to the 5,000 doctors of the province came to $330 million; by 1981-82 this had risen to $542 million; by 1982-83, watch it, the payout had risen by $142 million in that single year to the grand total of $684 million. It is true that the number of doctors grows each year by about 3 per cent and the patient population increases by 1.4 per cent. Still, I ask you, how can anyone justify an increase of $142 million (26.5 per cent) in the recession year of 1983 when poorer souls were in the straitjacket of restraint? Set that increase beside the less than $1 million that the B.C. Government "saved" in the same year by taking from 1,500 handicapped persons the $50 a month in expense money that they had been able to earn by doing community work. Biblical philosophy was being fulfilled before our eyes! "To those who have shall be given and from those that have not, what little they have, shall be taken away." How come Premier Bennett, our Strong Man of Restraint, overlooked an increase of that magnitude in medical earnings? Those dollars would keep open a lot of the hospital beds he closed down, shorten waiting lists and lengthen lives. Alas, the Premier is one of those right wingers who consider that income disparities, even such gross ones, are part of the natural order of things. And, what is more, he is not one to underestimate the political heat that the medical profession can bring to bear, especially in an election year, against those who challenge its dominance or its perks. That heat can be so intense, Legs, that even our indomitable NDP keeps its distance from the stove. Not for us either to chance a ruckus with that profession, perched on its political war chests and backed up by media personalities and hired guns (lawyers). And, as a last resort, doctors can threaten to strike, and that gives even the able-bodied a nasty turn.

Those payout statistics pose other puzzling questions because doctors' earnings have been rising faster than the increases in their fee schedules. Can it be that patients are being re-called more often than they need to be? And that they are glad to visit the doctor too often. Are hospital admissions being accelerated? Are drugs (proven to be safe but not necessarily needed) being too freely prescribed and needless surgery recommended?

Ah, I have been unforgivably forgetting Dr. Jory, who is standing by ready to provide more answers. The truth is that in his case a trained nurse with a decent salary could have examined those eyes with more loving care and attention at much less public cost (if the Statutory Medical Monopoly had allowed her to do so). If she were to spot a squint or a graver disorder, she would, I'm sure, have referred the eyes for specialist treatment. Similarly a salaried anesthetist without an M.D. to his name could put patients into a non-cost-plus sleep. So too could an ambulance attendant treat the body on the pavement; so could midwives make home deliveries (they do in the north, where doctors are far away, and women caring for women raise a crop of particularly fine babies). These "so coulds" apply very well to the sprawling field of psychiatry. The trouble is that doctors fight like tigers to keep outsiders off their turf, which should not surprise members of other organized groups who do the same thing, although seldom as effectively.

The Jory case also makes the point that the fee-for-service method of paying doctors can be at odds with the most effective health care delivery. That method fails to provide doctors with a monetary incentive to keep patients healthy, to treat them in the most economical way or to keep them out of costly hospital beds. On the contrary, it provides a disincentive to achieve these ends.

Once, Legs, to take an example from a related profession, I sued a dental surgeon over an unnecessary operation. My client was a young Chinese Canadian who went to his dentist for a checkup under his Dental Plan before visiting Mainland China. He had not felt a twinge of discomfort, but the dentist, although finding nothing untoward, nonetheless sent him upstairs with his X-rays to see the dental surgeon. In three minutes flat the surgeon prescribed an operation to remove wisdom teeth. Unfortunately, the promised three days in hospital turned out to be seven after a vein was carelessly perforated. After hemorrhaging subsided, my client slunk back to work still talking and looking like Jean Chretien. The point is that the decision to operate was made by a professional who had a financial interest in the outcome. Fee-for-service can and does lead to unnecessary, even harmful, procedures and treatments costlier than they need be.

Surely it is not beyond the wit of man to devise alternative ways to provide health care in which rewards come from health not illness, to compete for a while perhaps with the present system. This is hardly a novel proposition. There was a Chinese Emperor of the Ch'in dynasty who, when his celestial self fell ill, stopped paying his doctor on the grounds that the man was manifestly not doing his job. Yet the NDP is gingerly approaching the federal election (can't stand the heat?) under the banner of Defend Medicare. The Liberals' Monique Begin easily snatches that banner from our failing hands. Dammit, Legs, if we are bound to march forward into our glorious past we should know what that past was.

The achievement of Medicare by Tommy Douglas was only Phase I of the battle as he saw it.

As a youngster in Scotland Tommy suffered from osteomyelitis, which would have cost him a leg but for the kindly surgery of a doctor who operated three times without asking for the fee the family didn't have. Tommy went on to renown as a featherweight boxer and Premier, never forgetting. He made himself his own Minister of Health and by 1948 Saskatchewan had Hospital Insurance; by 1959 universal Medicare, in spite of a doctors' strike; and by 1967 the whole of Canada had followed the strength of his examples.

His Phase II preventive and treatment clinics, which featured salaried doctors and paramedical personnel, was blocked by the intransigent opposition of the Saskatchewan Medical Association. He could not find the doctors to enroll in the clinics; he imported some from England but they served only for a time. Those clinics—Phase II— remain our fight today.

But, alas, instead of fighting for Phase II, the NDP is big on more money for Medicare, 50-50 splitting of costs between Ottawa and the provinces (same taxpayer) and in opposition to user-fees as a tax on illness. No one can quarrel with these points, now or in 1959. Yet they are not hot items for sale on the hustings. A cost-conscious electorate wonders where the money is to come from, as indeed we should too. For our health establishment is developing a hearty appetite for bigger gobs of public money and is displaying alarming symptoms of elephantiasis.

To be sure, whatever the system there will never be enough dollars to provide every person and ailment with an infinity of treatment; choices will still have to be made; cost effectiveness will always be important to get the most from the health dollars; reform will have to be continual. Francis Bacon (not, by the way, one of us) said it better 400 years ago: "He who will devise new remedies must expect new evils; for Time is the Great Innovator."

With Phase II to win, will the NDP hug the shore rather than risk an engagement in deeper waters?

I'd like to see you enrolled in a Group Health Centre where the interests of physicians and patients were parallel and directed toward total well-being. Your centre would receive a state per capita annual payment; higher for an old fellow like me, lower for you, more recently weaned. The elected Council of the centre would make the money go further by doing its damnedest to keep you fit. Your fellow members would subtly keep you off the weed, and mine save my liver by counselling moderation. There would be psychological counselling for those who need it. Your minor dental pains would be alleviated by a trained nurse, a graduate, formerly of the Granville Mall. Everyone would have to have regular scans, and hypochondriacs and the desperately lonely would have an appeal to the Council in their quest for more attention. Some hearts and lungs would be contracted out to the big hospital on this hill, at the centre's expense.

Each year, a family or individual could apply to enroll in a different centre. The centres would compete with each other in patient care and, above all, in keeping their members healthy so as to have more money to spend on what ails them. Statistics would be fed into a Master Computer. Which centre keeps 'em alive and well the longest? Which has the lowest infant mortality rate? Whose counselling led to the fewest unwanted pregnancies? Which one dispenses the fewest uppers and downers?

And there's something else to be said for a health centre. Paying its doctor more than twice the salary of its head nurse would make neither good sense nor good manners, even if the doctor's training, at public cost, had taken much longer. Their comparable worth to the common enterprise wouldn't vary that much. Yes, those centres would fit very well into a fair incomes order of things.

I've got to pull over, my radiator is heating up. My aim

isn't to demolish the medical profession. Still, you know, long lifespans owe less to wonder drugs and medical treatment than to nutrition, decent housing, job satisfaction and relations between people that minimize the nastier kinds of stress. But even when our point of view is the one which runs the health system, we'll still be unable to produce a human internal combustion engine which will put the horse of health care permanently out to pasture. Our imperfect bodies are here to stay.

You won't let me pull over? You say that these proposals—salaried doctors in centres, fair reapportionment of wealth and income, and deferred consumption to provide seed capital for economic growth—will land the NDP in some awful ructions with powerful interest groups! Well, I'll ease your mind right now about that; they certainly will!

The ructions will be worse than the one Tommy faced with the doctors years ago. That's because the "me first ethic" of latter-day capitalism has encouraged group and private interests to squawk and buck in their own defence as if they were exercising a God-given virtue. Nevertheless, the NDP has to take them on where necessary and become the Candidates of the Hard Truth. If we don't, who will? Yes, we'll have the unenviable lot of having to disagree with quite a few dominant opinions and of trying to convince people that they are wrong. That will make for riskier politics and an uncertain success rate. All I can say is that it will not only be risky but probably suicidal to go at it without offering good alternatives. Go at it we must to win what we're for in the long run. The good alternatives will help us survive the battles.

We shouldn't underestimate our chances of spreading better states of mind regarding the problems of others. More people care than don't. "The sins of the warm-hearted man," wrote Dante Allighieri, "and the sins of the cold-hearted man, are weighed by divine justice in different scales.'' Dante should have added another test. It's no use being warm-hearted if, within your means, you don't help others by private and public actions. I won't fare that well by that text but am heartened to have known many who will.

Yours for Egalite
and Sante,

Alex

P.S. Couldn't we, Legs, have the words of Desiderius Erasmus (how I go for the oldsters) printed over the doors of our Health Centre? "Doctoring is better first than last." After all, he was, I'm informed, a closet socialist and the old fellow simply meant that where possible it's better not to get sick in the first place.

Alex Macdonald, Q.C., in ethnic regalia. From the *Advocate*, publication of the Vancouver Bar Association.

HEADS A.M.U.S.

Alex MacDonald, newly elected president of the Arts Men, who with his executive is busy planning the Arts Ball, to be held in Hotel Vancouver Crystal Ballroom this month. As usual, the "bigger and better" slogan is being used by the Arts Men to describe the ball.

Left: Alex gets "ink" in the UBC paper in 1937 and becomes addicted. *Above*: Wife and partner Dorothy Macdonald in 1944, the year of their marriage. *Below*: The author's father, M.A. Macdonald, Chief Justice of British Columbia and Honourary Bencher of the Law Society.

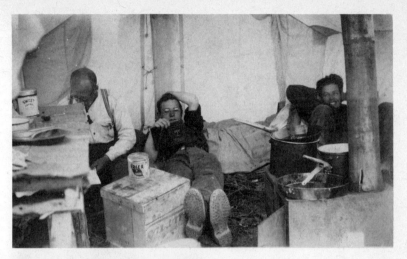

Above: After a ten-hour day of resetting telephone poles in the summer of 1938, the author reposes with a volume of Shakespeare in his tent above the Fraser River. *Left*: The author is introduced to a banquet of the Wong Society by his friend Quon Wong in 1977. In 1951, Quon Wong became a Notary Public in the City of Vancouver, the first Chinese Canadian to enter a legal profession.

Right: Indira Ghandi, late Prime Minister of India, meets her escort at Government House in 1974. *Below*: The "unofficial" opening of Vancouver's Robson Square, a project begun by the NDP and completed by the Socreds. The author, flanked by his secretary, Emily Chew, and MLA Gary Lauk, declares the Square open at ten to one on a warm autumn day in 1978. "Not ten minutes after I had the complex opened up, some guy came along and had the gall to do it all over again," said Macdonald, referring to the Premier.

Attorney-General Macdonald meets his match in Bobby Riggs, tennis champ and hustler, on the Empress Hotel lawn in June, 1975.

Left: Macdonald and MLA Bill King escort Dave Barrett into the House after his 1976 by-election victory. *Below*: Courtroom drawing portraying the author cross-examining Premier Bennett in the celebrated "scotch on cornflakes" trial in 1981.

THE CATS IN THE BARREL
WHO SEEM TO BE FIGHTING
MAY BE MAKING LOVE

The Legislature
Victoria, B.C.
September 21, 1983

My dear Legs,
    Last night I dreamt I was making a speech in the B.C. Legislature and woke up to find that I was. At four o'clock in the morning I took the Floor again to announce that it was almost my bedtime and moved "that this House do now adjourn." Voted down. The Chamber was a scene from the Beggars' Opera. Insomniacs sprawled, the virtuous snored and somnambulists stumbled about. Yours truly kept nodding off spasmodically, grateful for the speeches, fitful slumbers broken by the tintinnabulations of Division Bells. All night Sessions leave deposits of weariness in my bones. Who cares, the summer drones are over. I enjoy Parliamentary Confrontation. My disgruntlement has gone.
    All through the night we battle against Bill 3, which gives the government arbitrary powers to terminate employees in the public sector. At 4:45 a.m. the government ends debate on our motion to hoist the Bill for six months by invoking Closure. There is indignation in our ranks! Mr. Speaker rises in his Chair and ejects my fuming seat-mate, Dave Barrett, into the corridor and

under the television lights.

The debate goes on and questions file through my mind as they always do when we're on labour legislation. Are the trade unions so caught up in helping their own members that they don't care enough about income gaps in society as a whole? Do the unions care enough about evening out income disparities between groups of their own members? Are the unions ready to take some of the responsibility for making industry more efficient, or, for that matter, for making the whole economy run better? Are the unions, which have to speak primarily for their own members, and the NDP, which speaks for more people, on the way to a marriage breakdown? Above all, will the labour movement fight to replace the market system or be content to carry on its work within it?

These questions want answers now. Working people are being broken into three unfriendly divisions. There is a segment of relatively well-paid workers with job security and union conditions; then come the workers with high turnover, usually in less pleasant and lower paying service jobs; thirdly there are the unemployed, or grossly underemployed, with little enough of much of anything. This picture is buttressed by the fact that, on the average, the harder, less pleasant and less fulfilling the job, the less it pays.

I think about the six farm labourers in Tolpuddle, Dorset, England, who combined to form a union in 1834. They stuck together as a group to try to get a better price for the labour they sold in the marketplace. In this way they began to give practical effect to the principle of "one for all, and all for one." This principle collided with that of the market system which held, in Adam Smith's words, that "society will be best served when everyone cares for his own interest first." So the courts got into the act and sentenced the labourers to "transportation" to Australia, of all places, for engaging in a "conspiracy in restraint of trade.'' Socialists in the labour movement understand this conflict between two principles well enough but other trade unionists seem content to cut the best deal possible for their members while leaving the market system as it is.

Unions have been the strongest force behind wealth redistribution, minimum wage laws, social programs. Today they are low in public approval and not just because they are under attack and have a poor press; that's always been so. They'll stay low without new agendas; I'll be saying what I think they should be. With new agendas they will be stronger in the future than they have ever been in the past.

While my mind wanders, being keen in the wee hours, one of my ears catches the debate on Bill 3.

My colleagues and I gave that Bill a good going over and always give a good account of ourselves defending trade union rights. Deeper questions about unionism today do not, however, float to the surface in our speeches. Just asking them casts us adrift on strange seas of thought. It's easier to batten down the hatches and stow vexatious questions below with the ballast while our speeches berating the Government sail blithely on. We're like most NDPers who, out of loyalty to the cause of labour, decline to discuss the deeper problems in company. The discussions, if they occur, are confined to pillow talk, much of which I'm not privy to. I'm not as promiscuous as I used to be—in terms of party activism, that is. That blind loyalty is mistaken. Criticism and self-criticism is the only dependable ally of progressive change. And change there must be.

At 5:35, despite our valiant efforts, all speeches spent, Bill 3 passes second reading and I toddle off to bed. In any case, I have to add that none of my aforesaid weighty ruminations about union problems could have gotten in the way of our roundhouse attack on this particular legislation. Bill 3 whisks everyone back to the bad old days of firings at the whim of the boss. It strips away the security provisions that give job security to more than 200,000 public employees. Not that security rights are sacrosanct; no private rights are. Nevertheless they introduce a measure of fair play into the relations between employee and employer, making layoffs, terminations and promotions subject to length of service, competency considered, with rights of appeal to Boards of Arbitration.

Bill 3 goes beyond any powers Bennett needs to reach his stated objective, which is to cut the public sector. I sensed, we all did, something mean and vindictive in this legislation of his; as if Bennett, the little man who could not have got to the top without Daddy's help, was crying, "I'll show you who's Boss." Had he not, after all, brought his Cabinet Ministers to heel, even making their deputies report directly to him? Had he not made his backbenchers toe his line as the price of getting ahead or enjoying extra pay or the pleasures of junketing at public expense? And as for us, the lowly Opposition MLAs, how dearly he would like to trot us off to obedience school. One day, soon after becoming Premier, glaring balefully at us across the aisle of the Legislature, he was heard to mutter, "It took me just three weeks to train my dog."

There I go, Legs, into cheap political sniping; simply can't help myself. For Bill 3 does give a minatory message to those who work in the public service. "Keep your head down; don't be too active in your union; don't get into politics against the government; cut your hair short; your job is on the line." That's an intolerable affront to the dignity of employees.

So I fell on Bill 3 with a will; we all did. I didn't fall so heavily on Bill 2, however, another all-nighter, which did raise niggling questions. This Bill sets limits on wages and salaries in the public sector. No sooner was I up to speak against it than my little Doubting Thomas began to make a perfect nuisance of himself, tugging at my oratorical sleeve and whispering, "Yes, but . . ." Good political speakers drown their little men. Such speakers are often wrong but never in doubt. Note, Legs, I said good speakers; not necessarily the most convincing ones. For in every audience there are sceptics who sit scratching their chins, deeply suspicious of any message that implies everything is either black or white.

Bill 2 still allows employees to bargain through their unions and to strike. It simply confines any gains they may win in wages or fringe benefits within parameters laid down by the Cabinet. What, you may say, does that leave a poor public sector union to do to justify its existence? Not much, under our present adversarial system. But in the future, the kind of future I want, when unions actively participate in management, they will have lots of other things to do for their members. But getting from here to there? Oh, I admit that will not be easy, and in the interim unions will likely lose much, without compensating gains.

So my other self has a point when he whispers, "Why shouldn't these unions bargain within financial limits?" Why should big chunks of the provincial budget be drawn up under threat of a shutdown of some service the public depends upon? When capital threatens to strike by curtailing investment unless it gets the budget it wants, we like that not one little bit. (Of this, more later.) The less coercion on democratic choice by elected representatives the better. A budget, after all, is everyone's housekeeping accounts.

And, my little fellow whispers (shamelessly sounding like Bennett) that employment in the public sector is different; its jobs more secure (although a lot less so, thanks to Bennett), its services more essential. Can, he asks, nurses doff caps and strike hospitals? Someone might die! Can jail guards book off "sick" all at once? (Well, yes, I suppose, but only because the Mounties will not be far behind.) Can liquor vendors strike the drinking classes? That does seem terribly unfair, or so the topers tell me, but yes, the vendors can strike, for all the good it does them. Can grave diggers down shovels while bodies pile up like planes waiting to land at London Airport? Not always. Unburied bodies buried the Labour Government of Great Britain in 1979 and there may never be another one.

Nevertheless (get lost little man!) Bill 2 is bad legislation because it is discriminatory and concentrates too much power in the hands of the Cabinet. It singles out public employees for restraint while other employees, and everyone else for that matter, are allowed to go their best lick. (For the time being, Bill 2 is also a signal to the private sector to follow suit.) The nerve of Bennett! Here he is giving avaricious landlords carte blanche to hike rents (and turn down the thermostat) while curbing the incomes of a particular group of workers.

Now if this Bill 2 were part of overall restraints on excessive wages, salaries, fees, prices and profits, well, I'd be for it. And I'd be for it, further, because such an incomes policy would make it easier, indeed mandatory, to go after all ill-gotten gains—those of the tax evaders, of the insiders trading stocks on confidential information, of the oil companies acting in cahoots, of the whole caboodle of free loaders. And I'd be for it, finally, because unions will not survive as a significant social force unless they become partners with government and management in formulating a policy of work sharing and wealth and income redistribution. (Should unions say, "We'll just work with governments we like or that we helped to elect?" No, they shouldn't; they have a duty to work with what the people elect.)

I've run into good and bad unions. A good one started me on my distinguished career as a labour lawyer. That was in Windsor before you were begotten, or soughton, or thoughton, when I did some work for the Chrysler Local of the United Auto Workers. The UAW, under the leadership of Walter Reuther, was then turfing out its communist officers and forging a union that no one could say was just another special interest group. Reuther wanted the best he could get for his members in the existing society while always striving to get a better society for his members. He saw his members as workers, but also as parents, consumers and voters. I recall, as an example, how the UAW made total war on the discrimination against blacks in the work sites, which was epidemic in those days. In 1948 the Canadian UAW, on strike against Ford Motor, asked the looming, dignified black singer, Paul Robeson, to entertain one of its picket lines in his rich basso profundo. After he had performed, my wife accepted his invitation to return with him to Detroit to complete an interview for an article she was writing. UAW enlightenment was not shared by the immigration officials of those days. They were pulled over at the American border. Robeson had praised Soviet Russia for its lack of a colour bar; this, plus the sight of Blonde Pulchritude beside him on the back seat of a limousine, was too much for the border guards. "Get out, Robeson," they said and took him into their grilling room. After simmering for fifteen minutes, my wife boiled over and flew into the room like a dervish. Soon both were back in the car. "We don't call him *Mr.* Robeson here," a guard said in a parting shot.

But Windsor was so flat I couldn't see the scenery and not long after that incident I returned to B.C., where you can't see the scenery for the mountains. Here I began to turn a pretty dollar as a labour lawyer, which saved some plain folk from having their pockets picked by my tongue. Soon I ran into a bad union.

The social democratic unionism of the UAW contrasted with the business unionism of the International Teamsters. In 1954 the Teamsters raided the Fruit and Vegetable Workers Union in the Okanagan. My friends, Bob Smeal

and Jim Bury of the B.C. Fed, tried to stop this seizure of
bargaining rights of a Congress affiliate and made me their
legal eagle. They were almost too late. The 4,000 fruit
workers, getting in, at best, six months' work in the year
for paltry wages, had been demoralized by a losing strike.
Surreptitiously, the Teamsters had put the fruit workers'
secretary-treasurer on their own payroll and furnished
other officers with brand new Chevies. They had
dispatched fifteen of their bully-boy organizers to the
Okanagan from Seattle, mostly crew-cut former football
players, the Janizaries of the hoodlum empire. Before the
fruit workers' annual convention, they had already been
publicly proclaimed by the Teamsters as one of its own
chartered locals. On January 25, 1955, the convention
voted to ratify the fait accompli in the Prince Charles
Hotel in Penticton, while the three of us convened the
"true" convention in an upstairs bedroom, with the door
open. Nine delegates had the gumption to struggle in and
vote, by five to four, to counterattack on the ground and
in the courts. Bob and Jim slowly won the bare-knuckle
ground war while I retrieved the assets and bargaining
rights in court. I used the quaint argument that voluntary
associations can't change their basic nature even by
majority vote, any more than Presbyterians can vote to go
United and take the church hall, or a hockey club override
the minority to become a lacrosse club. Years later, I read
how the Teamster executive board had voted $500,000 to
re-elect Richard Millhouse Nixon and get Hoffa out of
jail. None of those dollars, I was glad to think, came from
the fruit and vegetable workers of the Okanagan. And
unlike the Teamsters, their collective agreements weren't
"front ended" to funnel pension deductions into
kick-back and pay-off pension funds. Since our skirmish
some of the Teamster locals in Canada have won a
measure of independence, with difficulty, always under
the threat of forfeiture of their assets and personal
expulsions.

Unions grew in power and influence in the 50s and 60s in an expanding economy. Those were the best of times for a labour lawyer (almost as good as they are today when the unions are in trouble!). Employers and unions fell into a rough understanding. If labour would keep to its own side of the table, it would have bargaining rights, grievance proceedings, and conciliation in the wings to settle strikes that got out of hand. Library shelves bulged with legal precedents. Even labour's losses usually left behind some incremental gains. Once, after losing a bad case before W.A.C. Bennett's Labour Board, we gathered at the door to read the decision. Fred Smelts, a member of the Board who always sat with a big mongrel of a dog on a leash at his feet, joined us to ask in his avuncular way whether everyone had met his dog. We allowed, yes, we had met the mutt, and we had read some of his decisions.

Tougher times and foreign competition, however, have brought the rough understanding to an end. Employers run to government with restrictive amendments to the Labour Code. More lockouts are declared than strikes are called. Labour slips further in the opinion of the general public, if there is one, with many seeing unions as a favoured elite defending past gains and rigid work rules. That shouldn't be surprising, for our so-called free enterprise system gives to the strong and leaves the weak to their own devices; where possible it breaks up working people into groups and individuals contending with one another. Under that system, and the adversarial way of bargaining that is part of it, there is bound to be a growing divergence between the unions, helping their own, and broad community interests.

Some gallant unionists met in Calgary in the radical days after World War I to make sure that everyone helped everyone else by forming the One Big Union. Ever heard of it, Legs? The OBU was to enroll the whole community as members, with its Constitution excluding only "Bankers, Lawyers and Saloon Keepers." What the devil

is wrong with Saloon Keepers escapes me. The OBU is long
deceased. Maybe even its dream. I suppose union and
other interests will always clash to some extent, even in a
democratically planned economy where everyone has a
union card and can pull a chair up to the table. The present
system, however, naturally engenders discord.

There's no point in asking whether the unions of today
are pressure groups for their own members or trustworthy
constituencies in the struggle for social justice. They are
both—within them are two tendencies striving for
supremacy. Labour has a monopoly face and a democratic
face. Some unions have more of one than the other, some
rank and filers have more of one than the other. For
unions reflect both the generous and the grasping instincts
of their members. The Canadian Worker, Oh, Legs, is not
some Noble Savage like thee; he is like me. At times he
goes hard for things that help everyone while at other times
he puts his own welfare too far ahead of that of others less
fortunate who have to pick up the tab. Now, don't take on
like that, because I said Labour has two faces. I've been
called two-faced myself and have to use Abe Lincoln's
retort that "if I had two faces, why would I be using this
one?" What matters is which face our grandchildren will
see. I'm betting on the good one.

I fondly remember cases I took for unions that
advanced, in some degree, the basic civil rights of all
working people. There was "Lucky" Macdonald, a faller
in the woods at Tofino, who in 1954 contended that what a
worker did in his spare time was none of the boss' business
unless it affected his work. We take that right for granted
today.

One morning his bullbucker ordered Lucky to work in a
rocky side where the trees were hard to get at. This
incensed Lucky, for he was paid by the volume of timber
felled and bucked. A furious argument ensued with his
bullbucker in the misty woods, with profanities freely

exchanged and ancestries impugned but no blows struck, ending with Lucky stomping off yelling, "We'll settle this later." That night a gala wedding reception was given for the logging superintendent's daughter in the community hall in Tofino. There, taking short leave of the bar, Lucky spotted his bullbucker waltzing by with elephantine grace. Cutting in, Lucky felled him with a single blow, leaving the bullbucker's lady friend standing alone with empty arms and a slack jaw. Lucky was canned and his union took up his grievance on the principle that no employee should be fired for what he does after work on his own time. Unluckily the arbitrator concluded that Lucky's lucky haymaker was "job related."

Not long afterward, however, the same principle stood up to save the job of a rigging slinger called McConnville. One late fall day his logging superintendent spotted a plump goose settling in on a small lake near the camp in the Fraser Valley. The superintendent promptly warned his crew that this goose was his to shoot for his own oven before the camp broke up for Christmas. McConnville, in defiance of the warning, stole out and shot the goose for his own Christmas delight, only to have his own goose cooked by being fired by the angry superintendent. McConnville laughed last, however, when the arbitrator ruled that this goose was not "job related."

Then, from the 50s, comes back a case where the Flight Attendants' union made another principle stand up, this time for the working woman. In those days, hard as it is to believe now, the airlines terminated their "stewardesses" (not their stewards) when they reached the ripe old age of 35 years. Entering into Holy Wedlock was another cause for early retirement. The companies wanted curvaceous young things in their aisles for the titillation of the ogling male pigs among their passengers. In court, we quoted a French Judge who had struck down a similar termination-on-marriage rule of Air France with the observation that if the poor things were fired for making it legal, "they would have to live in sin."

And then there was, memory holding the door, the Red Panties Case. Pacific Western Airlines had ordered its stewardesses (sic) to wear a uniform with generous decolletage blouses, mini-skirts and frilly red panties. Raunchy loggers, long pent in the Northern Woods, were beside themselves to order further rounds of drinks, but the blue-nose union, with my help, got the panties taken off after an arbitrator ruled that stewardesses were not Bunnies. (I'm treading lightly here, Legs.)

I've fielded injunctions for unions in strikes that left whole regions far better off, including its small store keepers, and even, dare I say it, the employers. In 1955 the lumber operators tried to break what little organization the IWA had in the northern Interior by refusing to give any pay increases over more than four years. The IWA struck back in a long guerrilla battle fought in bitter winter weather involving hundreds of scattered small mills and logging shows. Strike headquarters was in the basement of the CCF hall in Prince George and local command posts were tents in the snow (IWA organizers couldn't rent hotel rooms because operators were in league with the employers and to billet with a friendly woodworker was to get his name on a blacklist). I visited the tents to pick up some of the blizzard of Court Orders forbidding the strikers from doing this or that, and claiming damages against the union. The union won at last and rates and conditions in the north became standard with those on the coast.

Oh, yes, I've seen the down side too, where unions use their clout to demand gains that if available to everyone doing comparable work would keep the printing presses busy turning out dollar bills. Once, when I was the perfect image of a Cabinet Minister, I was on the receiving end of a nasty strike. The Office Workers Union went out against our NDP Government's pride and joy, the just-born

Insurance Corporation of B.C. Our Cabinet Committee, in a vain effort to avert the strike, had offered a fine package, too much really. There was to be a 35 per cent increase in salaries over 28 months; a work week reduced to 36¼ hours and more holidays with pay. This was not enough for the union, which insisted upon a 35-hour week made up of four working days. During the strike (which lasted three months) the union had a bunch of parading ninnies in front of the Legislature, and die-hards in the B.C. Fed pushed through a motion declaring that the NDP, whom they had helped to elect (and were now helping to defeat), had "lost the confidence of organized labour." "Defend us from our Friends," we ruefully thought. Other friends, among the voters, were slipping away, some unable to get a driver's licence or file an insurance claim, others annoyed that we had already offered the office workers too much.

I'd prefer, by the way, to see a 35-hour week come in by stages, on a more universal basis, under Hours of Work legislation. And my bones tell me that miners and sawmill workers should have it before, or as soon as, office employees in beautiful downtown Vancouver. A reduced work week without loss of pay represents a heavy cost imposition on any economy, unless it can be paid for from a good trading surplus or increased productivity.

Enough of the past Legs; present and future are what matter. And presently unions are in trouble in Canada, in the United States and in Great Britain. They are being assailed by a resurgent Right and they can't defend themselves and counterattack by simply soldiering along in the old ways. The troubles of the unions become ours in the NDP just as our troubles are theirs. We're each of us, unions and NDP, in need of a compass to find out where we have to go. Too few union members are fired with a moral commitment to union principles. There are cases of abuse of power within the House of Labour itself. One case is too many, for it gives all unions a bad name, especially when it escapes censure at labour's conventions. Labour needs the support of all working people. Unions are the guerrilla forces which, as our late Comrade Mao observed before he swam the Yangtze River, "can multiply in the warm feelings of the people as fish breed in the fructifying sea."

Seniority rights, for instance, are being used, on a larger scale than you might think, to give overtime rates to those who do not need the work or the money as much as fellow workers, employed or unemployed (with some companies, on cost-plus, using overtime to justify bigger profits). That would not have sat well with the Tolpuddle Martyrs who began a movement for equitable returns and work sharing. I give you a tale of two longshoremen. But first I'll tell you how I met them. You sent me to their homes. You were my campaign manager. Forgotten you haven't! Remember February, 1981, when I was far away as a guest of the West German Government? How a former NDP Cabinet colleague of mine, whose name escapes me, went hard after my nomination in Vancouver East as soon as I left town? Of course you haven't forgotten. You woke me up twice with expensive trans-Atlantic calls to Berlin: "Come home at once!" My situation was desperate. My quondam Cabinet colleague was spreading a rumour that I kept my clothes in Point Grey. Rumours about myself I don't mind, as long as they are not true.

The first longshoreman lived in a dilapidated street-level flat on North Templeton. Every morning he showed up at the hiring hall, lucky to get a couple of days' work in a week. Always at regular rates—no overtime. He was trying to support himself and his wife and child who were still in Quebec. He was a casual on the union spare board. Not for eight or nine years would he be able to join the union and vote at a meeting. Eight or nine years in which to behave himself, for the Old Communists control that union and prefer yes-men as members. Call him the underdog.

The second longshoreman lived in a fine house in the south of the riding, complete with all modern electronic paraphernalia. He even had a metal barrel which made as good a wine as if it had been old oak. As a union member with seniority, he was able to choose his hours and shifts of work. These were never day shifts at regular rates. Always premium shifts, with time and a half for afternoons, double for graveyards, Saturday afternoons and Sundays. His inconsolable wife was not pleased that he was so careless in his appearances. She seldom saw him! He worked seven days a week for months on end. His income? Regular rate $15.00 an hour—double is twice—use your pencil. Not an underdog.

Away back, before I reached my present years of indiscretion, unions used to object to overtime permits being issued under the Hours of Work Act because they wanted workers to be able to have the leisure of a good home life. Now I don't see unnecessary overtime coming to an end (employers like it too) until banned by Statute, so that others without work can have some of it.

Yes, I hear you saying my longshore example is an extreme case. You'll never get the grays right, Legs, if you don't know the blacks and whites. And anyway, I'll give you a good case, there are lots of them; a case of courageous union leadership fighting for social justice within the ranks of labour. In 1982 I was asked to speak to a meeting of the Vancouver IWA Local to extol the virtues of Social Credit as *I* saw them. That didn't take long and most members were still awake when I sat down to a burst of relieved applause. Then came the union business, and President Syd Thompson stood up to face down an angry group of his journeymen members. "You did all right last year," he boomed, "this year we negotiate for our lower paid brothers." That kind of stand takes guts. Those journeymen are articulate and more attentive to union business, and to union elections, than most of the members. It has generally sorted out that way in trade unions, as in the professions; the better paid members exercise more influence than their numbers warrant. No doubt that is why most union settlements in Canada have been percentage increases across the board which give more dollars to those who already make more, leading to wider differentials between lower and higher paid workers. There are signs that this situation is changing now, however, as more union members and leaders alike are recognizing the need for equitable income sharing.

As elsewhere, there is a battle going on within the unions —how to protect their own interests while steering clear of broader abuses.

Yes, there are some abuses, and much selfless action as well, in the House of Labour. That shouldn't surprise anyone. Still I can't help feeling how difficult it is to rekindle trade union principles of worker concern, for one and all, in our degenerate times when capitalistic values have seeped down from the board rooms into the work places.

There's more education in union principles in the labour movement today. It's needed. The other day on a ferry to Victoria I ran into a marine shop steward. Before long he was crowing to me about how he had bought the lumber for his house across the line in Washington State at a savings over B.C. prices in spite of the duty he paid and the lower Canadian dollar. I was surprised, not that he had shopped around, but that it hadn't occurred to him that I might be thinking that with a better union spirit he would have bought B.C. lumber to help our out-of-work woodworkers.

An electrician friend tells me that buddies of his (he, too, perhaps) sometimes finish eight hours of work at union rates and go on to moonlight for a non-union employer at

$10 below union rate. That's hardly an exhibition of concern for his union brothers with less seniority who haven't had work at either rate for some time. And yet it's hard for the union to check them up for acting in accordance with the norms of our acquisitive society. More union solidarity will come as unionism increasingly looks beyond the immediate material welfare of its own members.

Let me give you a short list of other problems facing unions today. They're insoluble until all of us achieve the triple goals of full employment, stable prices and equitable incomes. Those are goals, I have to add, that will come together, as one package, or not come at all. And, furthermore, you can't have any of them without paying a price. I'll get to the price by and by.

My electrician friend goes on to tell me that union rates and benefits cost contractors no less than $25 for an hour of work at a construction site. Still this is barely enough for a worker trapped in the expectations of a consumer-oriented society and faced with all the usual payments: the house mortgage, the car, holidays, the children to bring up; and it is less than enough for the tradesman who gets only six or seven months' work in the year. And looming over all the union tradesmen is the threat of the non-union contractor paying lower benefits and wages and steadily underbidding union employers for the building contracts.

The strike, labour's weapon of last resort, is becoming increasingly less effective. Sitting here in the Law Library, trying to give you more marbles, I watch pickets across the street shuffling around the B.C. Hydro building or taking their ease in folding chairs on the sidewalk. They've been on strike for weeks. Nobody pays any attention. Supervisors keep the lines humming, dreaming of the time off and extra money they will enjoy in Hawaii when the union has had enough. Other companies hire part-time employees who are harder to organize or to bring out in a strike.

Disputes over union jurisdiction intensify as work becomes scarcer. My car is on the same street, red flag in the meter. I haven't had a parking ticket for ages! Where have the meter maids gone? The maids, I begin to suspect, have been chased off the policemen's union turf. Not that policemen like to stop to ticket over-parked cars; but neither can they smother their feelings when others perform their constabulary duties! Unions (and professions), like the birds of the air, exert their territorial imperatives. And the maids stay home.

Silicon chips eat people. Overtime idles others. Alberta Wheat Pool, with 100 employees, installs the latest consoles. As a result only two new employees were taken on last year, although four were lost due to retirements and terminations. Nevertheless the grain through-put was substantially higher. That was in part because of the new devices, but partly for another reason, the scheduling by the company of more overtime hours for its work force. In this year's union negotiations, the grain companies are asking for the right to schedule up to fourteen hours a day of voluntary overtime. (They'd rather do that than have to pay fringe benefits to extra workers.) Everyone knows that technology makes the country as a whole richer. The trouble is that the market system does not translate enhanced productivity into a fair distribution of incomes and leisure.

Industrial union jobs disappear and lower-paid non-union jobs appear in the service businesses that are almost immune to union organization. Why? Well, economics is the main reason. A unionized fast food franchise, for example, has to compete with non-union food outlets with lower labour costs. McDonald's Hamburgers has more scampering non-union employees in Canada today than the United Steelworkers have members. I dropped into a

McDonald's the other day for my quarter-pounder and to do my research; I don't just make things up, you know. The scamp at the counter asked me if I wanted my hamburger "Win, Place or Show." What! Use the Macdonald name and offer me horse meat in a bun? Some half of the working class will be waiting on the other half. Glorious Free Enterprise continues to create jobs at the extremes of the range of earnings. I know what I'd do, Legs, to help organize low-paying service jobs if I were Law Giver for a day. My law would require all businesses to negotiate safety problems with an Employees' Safety Committee—a good start toward full union bargaining.

Watch some street corners to see a service trade which, should it exist at all, is most in need of a union and the hardest of all to organize. All weather working conditions and exposure to the winds of competition. No health plan to keep them in bed. No seniority system to give the older worker customer preference. Accelerated human depreciation without a pension plan. I started this paragraph half seriously and end it quickly before falling into a darker mood.

There's a graver problem to which unions must react realistically without having any ready solution. Productive jobs are being lost to cheaper labour in other countries, and the international union movement, try as it does, finds it almost impossible to organize the far-flung competition. National states themselves, in the closely knit world economy, are increasingly unable to protect their own industries. After the Armistice Day Parade I had a drink in the Legion with a Vet who had recently managed a ski clothing factory in East Vancouver. He had employed 150 women, who made only $5 an hour, with no union. This pittance wage was still too high to allow his company to compete with foreign imports, and now most of the women are drawing unemployment insurance, and some are on welfare. Most Canadian ski togs are now made in

Taiwan as our Cabbage Patch Dolls are outfitted in Hong Kong. Capital has no flag while labour has to stay put; capital flows to wherever subsistance wages, speed-up work and the absence of environmental controls yield the highest profits. We can't draw the shutters, with quotas and tariffs, because other countries need our dollars to buy our goods. Unions, with a real voice in economic planning, will have to be as concerned with cutting production costs as the boss; and in some cases, as the Garment Workers Union has done, even accepting a temporary reduction in wages. Nor can we lucky North Americans go on devouring the lion's share of the earth's resources; the trick will be to live better if less richly and work out plans so that when work is increasingly abolished everyone will be the gainer for it.

So here we are at the crossroads, with a toll to be paid on the path that will take us where we want to go. (Nothing's for free, as my friends who were born rich keep telling me!) Both unions and companies have to pay a price in giving up, for the most part, the dear old adversarial system of bargaining that underlies our present labour codes. And a great many people, some more than others, have to pay a price by recognizing that excessive economic appetites have to be put on a diet. These prices are well worth paying, for otherwise the road's impassable to an expanding economy that sells and buys abroad, with everyone working who wants to, for a decent share of what the country can make and earn. Can labour and the NDP hit it off well enough to educate, cajole and inspire sufficient of the public to pull this off together?

I had my doubts about labour affiliating with a political party. Yes, in 1961 I cried a little when the CCF wed labour in the Colosseum in Ottawa. Thousands of delegate hands were raised, on a hot, muggy day, to acclaim with a raucous roar the New Party. My hand stayed in my pocket. Maybe I was the first small "n" new democrat. I mourned the final rites of passage of the CCF into a tougher minded political party. I was afraid that what I liked best in the CCF would disappear from Canadian political life; the "conscience" to stand for what is right without counting where the votes lie. I even thought I would miss our dear old CCF "self-righteousness," that abiding infirmity of those whose hearts are pure! (Not to worry, Legs, we still have that in pretty good supply.) And I was afraid that the clarion call of Christian socialism to everyone who did not live by owning to come unto us would give way to the demands of sectarian interest groups.

I mourned but kept my peace. There was no just cause why unions and socialism should not be joined together. They are patible, not incompatible. We are meant for each other and depend on each other. A socialist society without a strong, free union component would be a nightmare. And in particular, by 1961 the socialist movement needed trade union dollars and organizers simply to survive as a national political force. (There were no income tax credits for political donations then; David Lewis wrested that from a minority Liberal Government in 1974. Today it is easier to get individual donations.)

The NDP has received the expected money and help, and its relations with its union bride have turned out to be free and open, for the most part, with no public spats, and no attempt by the unions to pack NDP conventions. Still I must say that our union partners are a mite touchy about any criticism, especially from NDPers. They figure, no doubt, that they receive enough of that as it is from companies and the press. At times it does seem as if union bashing has replaced hockey as our national sport. Moreover, our union partners are not inclined to brook any opposition on "labour issues" and that spells trouble because labour issues are also public concerns.

Something else spells trouble. The formal affiliation

with the unions costs the NDP votes that should be coming our way. A year after the new party was formed, even Tommy Douglas, the National Leader, lost his federal seat in Regina in his own Saskatchewan. There were and are simple souls out there who have concluded that the NDP puts the immediate concerns of labour ahead of their own; and still more who thoughtlessly identify every labour fracas or strike with the NDP. These election troubles will be with us until labour regains credibility as part of the national conscience by visibly accepting social responsibilities in equal measure with the exercise of its own rights. Then and only then will labour and the NDP have the power to oblige irresponsible capital to serve the public good.

You saw where J.K. Galbraith came to Ottawa last July; a lank, dour Scot, a famous economist and left winger. He didn't come to meet with the Canadian Labour Congress or our own bunch as you would expect. No, he came to meet with Cabinet Ministers of the Liberal Party, desperate for any breeze in their sails. "Dividing up the nation's income," Galbraith proclaimed, "is too important a matter to be left to the vagaries of the market." He made his pitch for a broad incomes policy, including controls on key prices, wages, fees and profits; not on all salaries and wages, just those in the giant, pace-setting businesses that escape the laws of competition; and not all prices, just the "managed" ones. Ah, those prices; even the auto makers, in the course of their amiable competition, manage to raise the price of your car when demand is falling. (The cats in the barrel who seem to be fighting may be making love!)

This matter of an incomes policy caused most of the fuss at our NDP National Convention in Regina this last summer. Our affiliated trade unions insisted that even the words "social contract" be kept out of our brave new manifesto. I know the unions feel that they were burned by

Trudeau's wage-price controls; but that shouldn't stop
them from promoting their own incomes policy and
certainly should not stop the NDP from having its. The
unions can't do our political work for us. The political side
has to lead and finally to decide. And deeper down many
of our friends in the labour movement want us to do just
that.

Too often, Legs, we in the NDP say what we think our
labour friends want us to say and clam up about what we
think our labour friends don't want us to say.

So where, oh where, is the NDP in all this today?

The NDP seems to be saying that we can spend our way
to full employment. We are not believed. The NDP also
seems to be saying that we can have full employment along
with unrestrained "free collective bargaining." Sensible
folk reject this too. They know that full employment
creates a sellers' market, for unions (just as unemployment
creates a buyers' market which business and others do not
hesitate to exploit). Without restraints (by voluntary
consensus or imposed by law), bouts of inflation inevitably
follow (which usually rob the poor and enrich the rich).
We can't have national planning for full employment and
plenty while wages and salaries are left to seek their own
levels, because they make up about 80 per cent of our
domestic, controllable costs. Leaving them out of our
economic planning puts us in with those Liberals and
Conservatives who try to cure unemployment with
inflation and vice versa.

I want the NDP to win public and trade union
acceptance of a new order of industrial relations. The
present head-butting adversarial method of settling
incomes is not working in the interests of working people
generally. Sure, some, with lots of clout at the bargaining
table, keep abreast of the field. On the other hand too
many fall behind, or don't have any table at all to bargain
over, and there's little today the unions can do about it.

And yes, I do want considerations of social justice to be the major factor in determining income levels. All working people should be able to enjoy an acceptable level of earnings, even if one sector of the economy has to subsidize another to make this possible. And, yes, levels of earnings should be as high as possible, subject always to the necessity of directing enough capital investment into plant renovations and useful new enterprises to provide reasonably full employment and increase the common stock of wealth.

And don't tell me, Legs, that I don't know how this can be done or how anyone can say how much a Judge, say, should make compared to a ditch digger. Hang in there, and perhaps I'll tell you, later. Sentient individuals know social justice or injustice when they see it, especially when the gap between the two tends toward extremes.

So while I have painted a pretty dark picture of how things are going these days I'm nonetheless optimistic that out of the nettles of danger socialists can pluck the flowers of safety. That new technology, properly used, can create the wealth to fund more life-enhancing jobs in the communities than the number it displaces, with everyone going home earlier. That closely knit world economy can provide an even richer interchange of products and techniques than we have today, although, as I have said, our productive industries will have to be leaner and fitter to stand up to foreign competition. No, don't let them put you and me down as the socialists who'll share their thirst with others if they will share their drink with us. In the controlled economy of World War II, with a national will to do it, Canadians made guns *and* had more beer, by sopping up the wastages of idle men and machines and cutting out useless activities that served no purpose except to make dollars change hands.

Before you untimely ripped me from my sojourn in Germany I had been talking to Klaus Richter, an officer of the German Central Union Congress. The historical development of their unions had been violently interrupted by Naziism. They were brought back to life in 1945 by Ernest Bevin of the British Trade Union Congress, who was also Foreign Secretary in the new Labour Government. Bevin was able to start with a blank page of history and he delineated seventeen economic sectors and provided that each should be represented by a single union. Bevin saved Germany's industrial future; his own country's he could not save. He gave the German unions a chance to advance toward the kind of industrial relations I have been talking about while the British unions still remain mired in their old ways.

I was full of questions to Klaus Richter, scribbling away at notes and asking my questions in broken German and English to which he replied in perfect English.

"Our labour militants say you're in bed with the boss, Klaus; that you have almost forgotten how to strike. Your wage gains are nothing compared to ours in Canada."

"Ah," said Klaus, "it's not the amount of paper in the pay envelope but what it can buy. Our unions have a hand in keeping prices down as well as the general level of wages, and other decisions too, such as capital investment, new product lines, etc."

"Well, sitting down with the boss in the Executive Suite makes you think like the boss, doesn't it?"

"Maybe the boss will begin to think like us. Our workers now elect half of the Directors in the steel industry and seek larger representation in all businesses."

"Still, Klaus, many socialists think that you are just trying to live with the system of bosses and workers instead of transforming it. What do you say to that?"

"We make speed slowly. Many of our young socialist Turks are as impatient as yours."

"Are the German unions pushing for public ownership?"

"Yes. The German Government now has equity shares in some 600 companies; 40 per cent equity in Volkswagen, as a major example. The steel industry is, however, still privately owned. In addition, our unions themselves have become major partners and owners. The construction unions have built 600,000 apartment units. Other unions have shares in shipbuilding, banks, retailing, fire insurance and other businesses. Isn't that public ownership?"

"Well, I don't know; union landlords may be as tough on tenants as private ones."

"Not likely when many of the tenants are union members, although I agree this is not co-operative ownership by those who live in them."

"What about the fiddles that go with industrial societies as they mature, cheating the sick plan, coming in late, drinking on the job?"

"Our top level Workers' Committees try to check these things. They appreciate that higher productivity helps working people. It's not a maturing society that encourages malingering but an unjust one."

"Only 43 per cent of your work force belongs to unions?"

"Yes, we do not have closed shops or union shops. Those who care carry the load for those who don't care. We do try to see that all who work in the various sectors of our economy—metals, food, construction and so on—get the basic wages and conditions that the unions negotiate for their sector. I know they should all be union members or at least pay dues, but we haven't pressed for a law to make that happen, not yet, anyway."

"Why don't your unions affiliate with the Social Democratic Party?"

"Unions have to deal with all governments. Still I can't think of any of my colleagues who are not contributing regularly to the Social Democratic Party."

I had a glimpse of the future, Legs, and it works pretty

well. At least Germany is—or should I say was—headed in the right direction. For that matter our CCF direction finders, 50 years ago, weren't far off the beam. The Regina Manifesto had this to say:

"Workers must be guaranteed the undisputed right to freedom of association and should be encouraged and assisted by the state to organize themselves into trade unions and share in the control of industry."

"Assisted by the state." This is where the NDP comes in. A new order of labour relations and equitable incomes won't develop by itself out of our go-for-it folkways. We either build it within a framework of laws, supported by a broad consensus, or not at all.

"Share in the control of industry." Kindly note that our Regina Bible said that unions should share in the control, not exercise the whole of it. Final choices belong to everyone through their elected representatives.

Time to knock off. I close by telling you how I'd go for it if I had my druthers. First I'd want to unearth for public viewing the facts about income distribution. In the 30s a Conservative Prime Minister appointed the Honourable Harry Stevens to investigate price spreads in Canada in response to outcries about the exploitation of garment workers. I'd want a wider investigation of incomes generally, the occupations, the job contents, the skills involved, the hardships, what comes just from owning, what's deserved and undeserved, not too much detail.

With the data assembled, and a clear understanding of the kind of social equality we are after, I would start with a pause in the growth of key incomes, prices and profits. The next step would allow those too far behind to catch up and would roll back those too far ahead. The techniques would include checks in key areas only, not of everything, and fair taxes on incomes and capital accumulations. And perhaps, why not?, the negative income tax, where many would get back more than what they paid. Of course this would involve additional public servants at various levels of government, but with unemployment being what it is I can't become too upset about giving people useful things to do. The costs of not doing it are measured in the billions, the wastages of unemployment and the ravages of inflation. And I close, finally, by saying, if I haven't already, that new labour relations won't and shouldn't work unless fair income policies apply to everyone.

That's all for now, brother,

Fraternally yours,

Alex

P.S. The Meter Maids are back in force and gave me a ticket. Scrub what I said about the Policeman's Turf. They're the last people I want to offend, and besides, one of them made me a grandfather.

'WE'RE NOT AGAINST THE TRULY NEEDY, THROW THEM A CRUMB FOR GOODNESS SAKE'

> The Court House
> Vancouver, B.C.
> October 22, 1983

Dear Legs,

Last Saturday I held court on a street corner while the Solidarity parade passed by. There were 60,000 marchers, so the papers say, cheerful in the strength of their numbers and also very serious about their mission—to save our social services from Bennett's economy axe. They were confident that the Socreds would have to take heed and restore the services; and determined, if they didn't, to take another step, already proclaimed on some of their banners, "General Strike! Stop Bennett's War on the Poor."

I surveyed the parade with musing eyes, wondering just what this massive demonstration really adds up to, and thinking of the unanswered questions they are leaving behind under their marching feet. Under my feet, too. "Where," to take the big question, "will the money come from to maintain and extend social programs? To create employment opportunities?" Legs, the turns of this old world are beginning to make me think. What a pain in the cranium that gives me. Are not Parliamentarians supposed to be exempt from the cares of thought? Will I have more questions in my mind when I finish writing to you than when I started?

I stand on my corner, smiling and bobbing as people come up, as easy with the crowd as the old stager who "hailed his friends and waved agreeably to his creditors." Some pass who are making their first political protest; they are more aware of government and what it means in their lives than ever before. That's all to the good provided it carries over into democratic electoral activity.

I don't share all of the high expectations of the marchers as to what this particular demonstration will accomplish. Some say hello to me with a hint of condescension, as one of the elected NDP MLAs shunted to the sidelines by Bennett's ruthless exercise of his majority in the Legislature. They feel that power is with their marching feet in the streets or on the picket lines, not in the halls of Parliaments. I haven't much faith in the Parliaments of the Streets. Bursts of energy for social change seldom last, although there have been notable exceptions. Power in a democracy finally resides and should reside in the ballot boxes, not in the streets or on the picket lines, however much from time to time these may influence votes and Legislatures. And certainly not reside, I need hardly add, in the board rooms, the corporations and in the lobbies of powerful pressure groups, where too much of it does today. What an old stick I am becoming! Yes, I give true-blue Winston Churchill full marks for saying that democracy is the worst system of government, except for all the others.

The Welfare State is under attack, and not just in British Columbia. Programs hard won in 50 years of struggle are being cut back or cut out: protection against the risks of joblessness, ill-health and disability; assistance toward the basic needs of shelter, food and transportation; cultural opportunities; all the necessities and amenities that the well-to-do can buy for themselves and the poor can't afford.

Social services and the socialist movement have grown up together, kids from the same block, each concerned that people should be able to deal with one another on a more equal footing. Now both are on the defensive.

We must have an understanding of how well the services have worked so far, not overlooking past mistakes, and what models can provide for their most effective delivery; how they can be paid for; the opportunities for consumer participation in the delivery of services where the recipients would have an interest in making the most of them and checking abuses; what needs and inequalities in the community demand the quickest redress; what services are necessities (such as day-care for young working mothers) and what ones are less necessary (such as legal aid beyond certain limits); and the whole ambit of services to people (I class publicly initiated job creation as a service). Finally, and above all, my dear Legs, we must have a clear definition of the principle we maintain in supporting government services to better let us get on with winning hearts and minds.

It's time to counter-punch, Legs, and to carry the fight to our adversaries; advance the principle that social services are the indispensable underpinnings of a free and equal society and not simply a regrettable safety net to save a few from intolerable poverty.

British Columbia is not an island entire unto itself; neither is Canada. Both are parts of an intricate world banking and trading order that is falling into disorder, with whole nations on the verge of bankruptcy. No Gnome of Zurich has to tell British Columbians that their books of account reflect the prices that our wood, coal, gas, fish and minerals fetch in the international markets. The number of our industrial jobs likewise depends to a large extent on prices on the international exchanges; and when these jobs fall off there is less revenue available to provide services and more demands upon them. You probably think I sound like the Board of Trade but I assure you that these simple truths help to explain why I am a socialist, not why I am not! I'll be back to this later on, and what to do about our export side. Here I'm concerned with the services themselves and how we can make a compelling case for their preservation and expansion.

The argument is needed all the more since Bennett and Co. have their own moral crusade going against us, maintaining that broad services to people undermine the moral fibre that enables them to take care of themselves. Of course, there's a lot of hypocrisy in that coming from them. It feels so-o-o good to have a political philosophy that conveniently suits one's pocket book; and I don't find those Socreds worrying about the moral fibre of the scions who live off the avails of their ancestors. Still, they are tossing serious questions at us that demand serious answers. They are claiming that dependency on the state is the road to tyranny; that the large bureaucracies administering the services sap the vitality of the nation; that the taxes to pay for them shrink the resources available to produce wealth in the private sector; that we are putting ourselves in hock. Thus they defend their tax and social spending cuts as a matter of principle as well as necessity.

I watched the parade wind slowly around the Vancouver Hotel where the Social Credit Party happens to be holding its annual convention. Inside, the delegates are giving Bill Bennett the greatest ovation of his career. Those Social Creditors, especially the loaded ones, see in him their own kind of guy; the eyes have it. Was not Bill a proud member of the Young Presidents' Club that met in the Four Seasons Hotel, a group restricted to millionaires under 40 with their own companies? They feel sure that he is not going to let public money find its way into the wrong hands if he can help it. The Revolt of the Rich against the Poor is in full swing. My imagination begins to play tricks and I picture some of the delegates near the platform, with

cracked voices raised in a plaintive anthem going
something like this:

We're not against the Truly Needy,
Throw them a crumb for goodness sake,
But don't forget the Truly Greedy
And give us Cake.

The picture fades and I'm back to pondering my
imponderable questions and thinking how simple the good
old fight used to be against Big Business and Greedy
Capitalists. Now I've concluded that capitalists do not
hold a monopoly on greed, they just lead the way. But it's
a ubiquitous weed that crops up here, there and
everywhere, and makes the NDP's struggle anything but
simple.

And to make matters worse, Bennett and Co. are
playing a winning political hand these days with their
restraint measures. I can take you to the home of a hard
hat in Vancouver East who doesn't mind saying why he
decided to vote Social Credit on his way to the polls last
May. Both he and the wife have jobs, each has a car, the
house is finally paid for, the children are on their own, so
they are doing pretty well. What he took exception to was
the NDP proposal to borrow $500 million to finance
municipal programs to put people to work. He tells me,
"I've worked hard for everything I've got. I'm not a
stockbroker. Why should I pay more taxes to support
'make-work' jobs to try to take people off the welfare
rolls? No way," he'll tell you, "are my hard earned dollars
going to put more bums to work raking leaves." No, Legs,
we can't put him down as meaner than thee or me. He's no
better or worse than others in a catch as catch can
environment. He can be turned around, I think, to vote
NDP again, if we can show him that everyone will be
sharing the burdens on a fair basis, which is far from what

is happening now.

I'd start by letting these marchers know that what they are after will not come about easily or overnight. True, many of them know that but it will give some a jolt. Not to worry if that's where the truth lies. For too long the NDP has soldiered along with promises of expanded social services and more funding to various groups without giving enough thought to the effectiveness of the programs or where the money can be found to pay for them.

I believe that the first priority of the modern Welfare State (at all levels) must be the provision of useful work at reasonable pay for the young unemployed coming out of the schools. This has become an essential demand upon governments because not enough jobs are or will be generated in the production of marketable goods or services. Yes, I know that the well-fixed have made "make-work" and "Big Government" into scary catch-words that all right-thinking people should accept as demonstrable evils. And indeed there are Tycoons of Industry and Finance who *want* an Olympic-size pool of unemployment as the only way they know to keep wages competitive, make workers hustle and keep the union in line. They'll be the last to embrace my incomes policy. Still there's no reason why "make-work" can't be efficient and useful and decentralized in its management; the social needs crying for willing hands are illimitable in recreation, the arts, forestation, clean-up and so on. Demonstrable evil is the compulsory infliction of idleness on young people in their formative years. Programs can be various; Roosevelt's Civilian Conservation Corps of the Hungry Thirties is one pattern, where young people blazed wilderness trails or cleared land for hydro dams or planted trees. Some projects, such as those for young people who have been cutting up because their lives have no frontiers to conquer or dangers to face, should be under former Sergeant-Majors who know how to bark orders.

I pick out the young jobless as the parade passes by without being able to think or feel in their skins. Few politicians can do that and my life has been too cushy. Yet I've seen enough of the young people hanging around job sites or calling at union offices or lining up outside of church basement halls to be able to imagine the ebbing of self-respect, and, yes, the suppressed violence. Statistics measure the spillover costs in rising rates of youth crime, family break-ups, hospital admissions, suicides.

We share a friend, who shall be nameless, not all that young anymore, who has never had a regular job. A doctor recently presented him with the name of the cause of some awkwardness in his speech and manner—dyslexia. He has some, not much. He is bright, no doubt about it, for occasionally we read the same London *Observer* and he gets more out of it than I do. But a hot seller on the job market he is not. I tell him that he's better off than many others, with his handicapped allowance, and all the voluntary things he's into. No use! He pines for a job, the satisfaction of earning his way.

Another friend finished teacher training two years ago without being able to get a teaching position. Now she is thinking of leaving for Arizona where the starting teacher salary is $12,000 compared to almost $25,000 here. Teaching should be labour intensive, for how can one teacher relate to 35 tots? The Teachers' Federation is militant in support of its unemployed members but not sufficiently ready to assume its share of responsibility in work and income sharing.

On a windy, rainswept night I picked up a young business woman on Davie Street; *not* what you are thinking! After solemnly agreeing, in both official languages, that her business time must be paid for, we repair to a restaurant for coffee and doughnuts. She's twenty, vivacious, bundled against the cold like a mummy. She tells me she is one of twelve children from Shawinigan

Falls on the St. Lawrence and inquires solicitously about my family. Very important, she says, especially when you are so old! Does she look forward to marriage and children? "Of course," she replies, "definitely in my future." Does she know the local boy from her hometown, Jean Chretien, with his gambler's mouth? "No, I'm not into politics." Her first job was in a boutique in Montreal, not really enough to get by on and after a while she began to serve different customers from time to time. Then came the flight to Vancouver with no idea where she would rest her head. I think of her esprit at less than one and twenty, and of a lot of goodness, whatever may be thought of her calling. Did having too little to rent an apartment cause her to fall into sin? No, poverty alone didn't cause her to choose that calling but she would have chosen a different one with better earning prospects.

I'm in no mood to hear some dingbat tell me that better social services, decent affordable shelter and income supplements for the working poor will ruin their morals, young or old, and make them lazy. I don't want to argue the point; just don't want to hear it.

No, there won't be a General Strike. The trade unionists, who helped to organize this demonstration, will patch up their agreements, and stick with the jobs they are more fortunate than a lot of other people to have. The organized will remember the poor and the unorganized (now I'm really in a cynical mood but I'll say it anyway) a little like the Gambler's Lady remembered her Man. When he was cleaned out after losing the big pot, he turned to her and asked, "Do you still love me?" "Of course I do, honey," she replied, "and, honey, I'll *sure* miss you."

That's the cynical view. Of course groups and individuals watch out for themselves, but there's more to it than that. There's a great deal of altruism among these countless thousands of marchers, unionists, teachers, mothers and jobless, or they wouldn't be out here today. I discern a longing, especially in the young political neophytes, for a cause that goes beyond their personal needs, a willingness to sacrifice if need be so that all British Columbians can share in the good things of life. In that lies challenge and danger for the NDP. If we don't provide the cause others will, or what's worse, these protesters will lose faith in the political process. How then do we confront the danger and accept the challenge and get back on the offensive so that we can carry a common cause into the camps of our enemies and burn their tents?

Again, jobs, but without economic planning there will not be enough of them to expand the industrial and commercial sector. Nor will it be feasible to set out labour intensive employment programs as public services designed to meet social needs and conveniences. If this means many more public dollars, as it does, the question arises more insistently than ever, where will the money come from? That's the billion dollar question our adversaries don't expect or want us to answer.

Leaving big industry and finance aside until later, time and we willing, there are lots of unproductive dollars that must be signed up or conscripted to do a decent day's work in the public interest. Allow me to dip into our past and give you a quotation (our critics just love to say that NDPers always look backward when they are in trouble, blind wretches that we are). Fifty years ago the seers who wrote our Regina Manifesto called for "a drastic extension of . . . inheritance taxes." Only one of our seers survives, as far as I know, the gentle Poet and Teacher Frank Scott, his flaming bush of a conscience still burning brightly. Inheritance taxes have not survived at all, wiped out, province by province, and then nationally, by the lobbies of the rich.

Oh, how they gull us with the comfortable illusion that Canada, after all those goody-goody Liberal Governments, is a middle of the road social democracy. But I'll bet there's not a western country, Banana Republics apart, with greater concentrations of wealth in fewer hands or lower incidences of taxation upon upper level wealth. And now the Pearly Gates are totally toll free—all men are cremated equal!

W.A.C. Bennett resisted the abolition of inheritance taxes in British Columbia. (They were called Succession Duties and were far from being drastic unless you died an unlucky bachelor without children or kin). He liked the jingle of coins in his till in Victoria, hardware merchant that he was. And I suspect that the boy from the backwoods of New Brunswick who became Premier had a care in him for those born outside of any charmed circles and without a silver spoon. His voice still echoes in my memory. A night in the Legislature, in 1966 I think, W.A.C. erupting, in short emotional bursts (he never finished a sentence unless he was reading something), rebuking those of his MLAs who were not willing to give an even break to those babies who had not been shrewd in the choice of their parents.

I sprang to the Old Man's defence, even more emotional than he had been, getting off lines like, "We do not believe in a hereditary aristocracy of wealth; we believe in equal starts for one and all in a fair race of life." So pleased we both were when the debate was over, in ourselves.

All the while money kept whispering in the corridors of power. By 1971 W.A.C. gave in and promised that Succession Duties would be abolished. His money bags were threatening to take up their holdings and plunge, like Gadarene Swine, over the steep rocky mountains to perish in death-duty-free Alberta. Others declared they would die in the balmy Bahamas, never suspecting that this would prove to be as close to Paradise as they would ever get.

The Old Man was defeated before he carried out his promise but sent back a sprig from his trunk in Bennett the Second, who eliminated the duties with relish and alacrity in 1977. The surviving NDP MLAs fought the repeal both as a matter of principle and as a matter of revenues, for the duties, modest as they were, brought in close to $50 million a year. We duly congratulated Premier Bennett on having himself become a millionaire in only two generations, instead of the usual three. And we totalled among ourselves the best estimate we could make of how much the wealthy Socred Members in the Government benches would save, this or that side of the divide, in voting against inheritance taxes. In return, we were stigmatized as grave-robbers and then stroked with noblesse assurances that hereditary fortunes at the end of the day trickled down to benefit the common people, as crumbs fall from a well-laden table.

I have no trouble in thinking of other dollars that should be enlisted in the people's army. The techniques to put them to better use are not beyond our imagining. Behind the stories on the financial pages you can have a look-see at a veritable carnival of greed, with various stalls on its midway, where private fortunes are made without any discernible benefit whatsoever accruing to the public. Corporate take-overs, for one, have become a popular gambit, with both raiders and losers profiting handsomely as stock prices are pushed up in the interplay of bids and counter-bids. The profit-heavy chartered banks help both sides with loans, careless that they could do the community a better turn by using their depositors' savings in other directions. Take-overs do not generate any new jobs, unless among lawyers and tax experts. And it seems to me that those who take over corporations have less concern for the health of the enterprise that do those who lose control. The takers are like the farmer who was interested in his chickens; of course he was, but he was interested in them for what he could get out of them.

Now I turn, casting about for other unproductive dollars, to the private capital gains accruing to individuals or companies who receive a public "right" or franchise from government. For example, governments give out liquor licences with a stroke of the pen. These soon become valuable salable assets. The value should accrue to government coffers but it does not. In the days of my glory I introduced legislation in 1974 to license some genial water-holes known as Neighbourhood Pubs (after some arduous research in the form of several pub crawls I endured in the City of London). Some friends of mine applied for and received one of the pub licences, all on the up and up. Now that licence, or "right," has a marketable value of some $300,000 over and above the facilities of the pub and ordinary business goodwill. That value has been created by the consumers, largely the congenial young of tippling dispositions, and it seems to me that the whole of it should be recaptured for the benefit of all of the public when the pub is transferred or sold. Our NDP good intentions were to see to this by companion financial legislation, but before it was approved, a funny thing happened to our government on its way to the polls in 1975 . . .

I could put you into a fast sleep, Legs, by listing the different public franchises in private hands that swell in value with the effluxion of time: mineral rights, taxi licences, timber grants, turkey quotas. Ah, yes, the Turkey Quota!—where a portion of an exclusive market in legs, wings or livers is granted to a particular producer who still calls himself a farmer. Don't get me wrong, I support the principle behind our Marketing Boards, for otherwise the producers would be exposed to cut-throat competition among themselves and I think that they and their hired hands have as much right to fair remuneration through measures of self-protection as plumbers or lawyers. To be sure, Marketing Boards mean that we pay more for our food products. We pay in Vancouver, for instance, $1 a pound for a turkey that costs 29 cents a pound on sale in

Los Angeles. We should pay more but not that much more. That $1 represents more than a good return for bringing the turkey to market. A good part of it goes to making the Turkey Quota, which the public gave out for nothing, a valuable trading asset in the hands of the producers.

Taking another trail in the same direction, I recall an agronomist deposing in 1977 that the value of an acre of land in Richmond rose from $30,000 to $250,000 when released from our Agricultural Land Reserve. I fail to see why capital gains resulting from the rezoning of land should not belong to the state, all of them, not just a part under the capital gains tax, with all of its escapes and deferments. Old MacSpetifore had a farm, and in 1979 he left a closed Committee meeting of Cabinet Ministers, along with some Socred cronies who had also been privileged to attend, with a Paper worth instant millions. The Paper released 600 acres of his potato land in Delta from the Agricultural Reserve. (Some of the first potatoes in Canada were grown on that very plot of land.) He took the Paper to banks and trust companies and raised mortgages of no less than $155 million against this land. Its previous assessment for purposes of agriculture: $600,000. Now you may say that this example should be set aside for study by students in a School for Scandal. Nevertheless, it illustrates the magnitude of the private gains that usually follow the public up-zoning of land and gives you an idea of the shelter costs to those who will one day occupy the townhouses on this particular acreage.

I'm told (without undertaking any enjoyable research) that the centre of the City of Stockholm is municipally owned and let out on long-term leases to buildings and commerce, with the rising values brought about by a growing community falling in the fullness of time into the hands of succeeding generations. This causes me to ponder as I watch the elevated track bed for Vancouver's new transit cars slowly stretching like a white concrete snake across the city. Passenger stations are spaced every mile or two, some of which will be surrounded by busy commerce. Now I ask you, why our good Socialist Mayor Mike Harcourt (fractious as his Council is) should not have demanded that the land around the stations be taken into the public domain by purchase, expropriation or strict zoning measures so that their capital appreciation would accrue to the city instead of to private speculators? Should NDPers wince at the slightest signs of voter resistance or cower before the shibboleths of the influential when the sacredness of private land ownership is raised? It's not that our civic amenities in Vancouver (roads, parks, museums) are that badly under-funded now compared to those of other cities. It's the direction we are headed in that bothers me. I wander in some of the big American cities where private affluence abounds alongside public squalor and think that's us, tomorrow, if we don't do something about it.

Oh, Legs, could you and I with Fate conspire, to grasp this sorry state of things entire, the good earth would still be in communal ownership. There'd be leases of 99 years duration to accommodate those who pay terrestrial visits and who then, one by one, creep silently to rest.

To regret, to dream, no more. Private home ownership is embedded in our folkways. We can, however, wring speculation profits out of the costs of shelter. The flipper buys and sells homes and apartments; mortgage discount businesses prosper; the real estate dealers exact their 5 or 7 per cent on most transfers; all profits and commissions that derive from the provision of housing are added into the prices people pay to put rooves over their heads. Not that housing should be a money-maker for government (apart from the profits of rezoning); the objective is to make it cheap. So I'd take the flipper right out of the housing market and dry him out by taxing the whole of his ill-gotten gains.

Oh, we had a fine example of the flipper's art, admittedly a horror story, not long ago. Nelson Skalbania, who prefers to use other people's money (including the tax department's) when he buys and sells merchantable items such as baseball teams, purchased a retirement home with 162 units called Crofton Manor. The price tag: $10 million in 1981. (This gave the vendor, a Vancouver lawyer, a pre-tax profit on this sale of $6 million.) Skalbania paid the big price of $10 million because he intended to turn the property over in short order for $16 million. To do this he converted the rental units into condominiums; then he gave the old folks six months' notice to get out of their apartments, unless they could afford to buy them, which, of course, they couldn't. I don't think Skalbania made what he expected out of this flip, but profiteering of this diverse kind in dwelling units is far from uncommon in Canada.

I've been in apartments, financed by a government mortgage, that should never have had a building permit. The walls were so paper thin the residents couldn't make love without their neighbours. Some had no windows at all. Alderman Harry Rankin describes them as "three dens and a living room." Why, when the public puts up the main financing, shouldn't the public own the land? And get the benefits of growing land values?

Profiteering extends beyond the realm of dwelling units and takes in even the convalescent beds of private hospitals. The bed bought for $5,000 may, with the help of the taxpayers' dollar, be sold for $30,000 in a few years' time. What do you suppose our forerunner, the Prophet Isiah, would have thought of speculation in the provision of housing? Not much would he have thought of it, the irate old fellow, for he declaimed, with a few huts in mind, "They shall not build and another inhabit; they shall not sow and another reap." Too far to the left he was for me, but what indignation!

As for real estate commissions, I've made speeches, and

even put a flea in the ear of His Worship Mayor Harcourt, proposing municipal home exchanges. My exchanges in City Halls would give buyer and seller the option of dealing directly, with the help of a friendly computer printing out the latest information on comparable values, zoning, services, charges, all for a modest fee. No one pays any attention. Yes, this would displace a few sales jobs but I hold that, while other labour intensive services are called for, the object in housing must be the lowest possible costs. For housing, like health and education, is one of the mentionable staples of life.

I'll digress to give you an activity that should not be a money-maker for governments. Oh, something in my bones murmurs against governments, as if they were midway barkers, hawking lottery tickets. I went so far as to break with my colleagues once to vote against $580,000 for devious advertising to sell Provincial Lottery Tickets. It's partly because lotteries are a tax on the dreams of the poor, the credulous and the desperate; but mostly because the value system they represent is precisely what socialists are against. Say what they will, and they will, socialism is not something for nothing. For real needs and for services rendered, yes; for tax-free bonanzas from Lady Luck, no. The present economic order spills out too many benefits that are neither earned nor deserved, often to the shifty, the lucky, the well-born. None of what we stand for will work without an accompanying turn-about in values.

We can find lottery moneys elsewhere. Higher income taxes on the upper brackets is an obvious place to look. Sales taxes should be looked at too. Why not graduate upward from its 7 per cent the sales tax on the sleek pelts of animals and allow wild things to breathe more easily? Taxation on the ability to wear! Or on other articles of conspicuous expenditure with less practical utility than ability to impress the Joneses: cream Cadillacs, gleaming white yachts and Gucci shoes? Would not these affluent devotees thank us for increasing the differential between the priority of the luxuries they display and the necessities others get by on? Or would they be distinctly annoyed?

I want the breaks to come from merit. Last January the teachers of Maquinna School in the East End asked me to tell the story of Robbie Burns on his birthday. There to greet me in the gym was a United Nations of gamins, shining faces, curious eyes, the sons and daughters of labour and poverty. Awash with children, resplendent in my kilt and regalia and preceded by a piper, I was accosted by a pert miss of six and a half years who rolled her saucer eyes over my knobbly knees and craggy beauty to ask, "How long have you been in this world?"

How many, I wondered, of these children will climb the rungs of the ladders to positions of status in the professional and business worlds? Fewer than from the children in more affluent areas, but more, I agree, than in times past. The invisible power of money remains a screen through which too few of them will be able to pass regardless of dedication and ability. Sense and worth are still depreciated coins in the market place of life. Arbitrary handicaps and head starts are too common. Yet to come is the time when individuals are honoured and rewarded for what they are rather than what they have.

Ah, me, another point or two and I'll sit down. Why should socialists contend that social programs be both cost and service effective? Can't we leave it to those on the right, who couldn't care less about the services, to make noises about "welfare fraud" and other alleged abuses? No we can't. Unless the services are well administered they won't inspire the voter confidence upon which they depend. And, besides, the dollars saved by running economical social services can be used to meet other needs.

There's an insidious law that says that work expands to consume the money available. Take legal disputes. Show me the case that won't go longer and higher when fees are in good supply. So, in our legal aid programs, we have to try out new models of service delivery. We could use salaried public defenders to act for most of those charged with offences to make our legal aid dollars go farther. We could have duty counsel at the doors of the criminal courts, and mediators in the civil courts, to give citizens an inexpensive perspective on their legal predicament and what costs they should or should not be in for.

How can Pharmacare be kept under reasonable control in our drug reliant society? There's no end to the demand for prescription drugs, and kindly physicians are glad to write the prescription and bill the plan. For one thing, we should manufacture generic compounds in public labs to meet the needs at less cost. For another, there can be public education in how to keep the body humming as naturally as possible. We can't, however, pass a law to make people walk around the block to ease their aches and pains without any chemicals!

Am I beginning to ramble, Legs? (Beginning?) Mind and pencil in a paper chase, both in need of sharpening? Something else. More things should be free! Well, I'll take that back; nothing's really for free. I mean that more things should be freely available to everyone by being paid for in common. As a matter of democratic choice. Education, health, parks, are mostly free, in that sense. Why not nourishing school lunches, bus rides without a meter to feed, or phone calls without a quarter in the slot? Just think. Five hundred years ago Salvation was for sale in the form of Indulgences. Now it's free! I want to reduce the power of money by limiting the number of things money can buy. And, yes, elections should be among the things that can't be bought.

I've come to the last question I asked myself. What is the principle behind social services? Why should those who work support those who can't or don't get the chance? "From each according to his ability, to each according to his need." You've heard that one, Legs, but I'll bet you don't know where it comes from. I found the place, naughtily browsing beside my wife in St. James Church when I should have been following the service. The King James Version relates the story of the Householder.

At break of day the Householder sent labourers into his vineyard after promising each a penny in wages. He sent out others, still idle in the market place, at the third, the fifth, and some as late as the eleventh hour. At fall of eve all the labourers got one penny. That was hardly a case of equal pay for equal work! Naturally, those who had borne the brunt of a full day in the sun complained that they should get more than the late-comers.

The Householder replied that they had received the penny they had agreed upon. As to what the late-comers got, he added, mysteriously, "I can do what I like with my own money." Men of substance take those words as support for property rights, but that's not so. The Householder was simply asserting his right to treat them all fairly. He was really saying that the early-birds and the late-comers alike had families to support, all had been willing to work, and all, therefore, should get the same.

A revolutionary powder-keg of an idea, Legs! In spite of its age! Too good, you may say, for this peccant world. Yes, I suppose it is. I have come to accept that economic and social measures can advance together only with advances in people's concern for others. And I can add this. I did detect in the Solidarity Parade a growing political constituency of the reawakened social conscience where lie the votes that should be ours.

Now I will take my seat. The Wonder and the Wormwood of it all are too much for me.

Solicitously yours,

Alex

A FAIR TRIAL IN THE COURTS
WHILE MANY ARE SENTENCED TO DEATH
IN THE MARKET PLACE

The Court House
Vancouver, B.C.
December 10, 1983

Dear Legs,

I'm in the Law Library again, pencil and cigar. The Hydro pickets are across the street. I have another ticket from a Meter Maid (this time I saw her; some chic she had) and I'm back from a mind-spinning experience in Los Angeles.

Are you ready for this? There I was in the City of Angels, an expense-paid delegate to the North American Conference on Religious Liberties. Imagine that! Me, an infidel, in the midst of outlandish cults and sects, many I'd never heard of. (My friend Wesley Wakefield of the Bible Holiness Movement got me there to speak for the "laity.")

My fellow delegates were there bucking for all the religious freedom they could get, or get away with. They kept saying, ad nauseam, that the First Amendment to the American Constitution guarantees religious "rights" for as long as the country lasts. That means, they said, that governments not only have to keep hands off their beliefs, which is fair enough, but also hands off any money they could loosen up from the pockets of people who could be inveigled into parting with the filthy stuff.

No wonder the question of "rights" is still rattling around in my head. It's about time. I've written enough about social obligations to lose half my friends should they find out what I really think. Perhaps I can lure some of them back by talking about rights they've got coming to them. A right is simply something that if you don't have you can go to a judge and ask him to get it for you. But just *what* he will get for you, in any given case, is a more complicated matter.

Last year's Charter of Rights not only enshrined the words "freedom of religion" but a lot of other equally ill-defined rights as well. The NDP drifted into supporting that Charter with very little discussion about what we were getting into. No wonder we almost shivered our timbers, and not just because the Charter entrenched two official languages. We also split because some NDPers believed that the Charter was taking too much decision-making away from elected representatives and giving it to the judges. Only the future will reveal how far the judges will intervene in cases that are more of a social than a legal nature. The judges themselves will set the benchmarks of judicial decision-making.

To take a harmless example, consider a jail that is overcrowded, with prisoners double-tiered in single cells. Since the Charter now proscribes "cruel and unusual" punishment, a judge could order that the prisoners be released or order the public to build a new jail. Or, again, a judge could decide, under the same words, that the death penalty had to go regardless of public opinion. We can live easily with either of those decisions but there are two sides to judicial coins. The same court might also strike down legislation which redresses social injustice by redistributing wealth. You say that won't happen, Legs? I have it on the highest authority (from my own brother, the Judge) that all judges are not socialists.

These days the land is loud with cries for various rights:

Prisoners Rights, Gay Rights, Aboriginal Land Rights, the Right to die with dignity, the Right to do what you will with your own body (even if it is tenanted), the Right to health, to property, to a lawyer, the list goes on.

It so happens that most rights impinge in some way upon the rights of others, and that many rights are quite empty unless the person wronged has enough jingle in his or her pocket to take advantage of them. Other rights are not legal rights at all, but social and political questions involving the allocation of scarce dollars in the best interests of the community.

No way can the NDP close its books on this question of rights just because they are now embedded in the Constitution. Rights are too important to be left to the lawyers. Rights and so-called rights will keep showing up on court calendars and on political agendas for years to come. No wonder this whole thing hit me where it hurts, in the vacuum between my ears, last week in Los Angeles.

The Conference on Religious Liberty met in the same hall in the Ambassador Hotel where Bobby Kennedy fifteen years ago left his cheering supporters to pass through the swing doors to the kitchen where he was shot. (Can you imagine a more ghastly affront to human liberty than the "right to bear arms" as interpreted by the American courts and Congress?) Bobby Kennedy would not have been comfortable with the lot I fell in with. He inclined toward governments reaching out to bring social and economic opportunities to the common man. My fellow delegates were full of jargon such as "getting governments off the backs of the people." I was an odd dissenter, with only one or two sympathizers, one being an Episcopalian from Toronto who was as shaggy as I was.

The Moonies got the mike first to complain about a grievous breach of their First Amendment rights. Their Reverend Sun Moon had been convicted of tax evasion and a pride of lawyers was profitably engaged in his appeal. Somehow $1.6 million had found its way into the Reverend Moon's personal bank account. The Moonies said that this was church money and the interest on it was tax exempt, with the state not entitled to so much as a peek at it. But a puzzled old judge wondered how in the name of Sun Moon the money had come to be, and gave his Reverence something to think about. He gave him time. I would have too.

Freedom of belief, association and expression should be among the inalienable liberties of mankind. However, there is a business side, even with churches, that should be subject to public scrutiny. Legislators can decide to grant churches tax exemptions as a matter of popular choice. Even then, insisting on hiding the books, as the Moonies did, is a denial of the public right to know. Sadly, I concluded that the Moonies were more busily engaged in the service of Mammon than of God and that the tax-man certainly should have knocked twice.

Then the Hari Krishnas lodged their complaint. They had been stung by a biased jury with a far-out $9 million in damages for using "coercive persuasion" on a fifteen-year-old girl. Lawyer Guttman of the American Civil Liberties Union rose to identify this case as a plain violation of First Amendment rights. The girl's mother would not have agreed. She had searched for her daughter among the Krishna centres as if trying to find a pea that was never under the same shell. Alas, most of the delegates thought more of sect than mother's rights. (Come to think of it, few if any of my fellow delegates were women.)

The Scientologists moved about, quietly working the crowd, in neat shirts and ties, always polite. My wife asked one of them about the story of a woman who had been beaten for not observing the strictures of some cult leader. It seemed that her husband, who was not in sync with the sect, had made something of a fuss about it. My wife received the reply, "perhaps she needed to be beaten."

Cults and sects will multiply. The times are ripe for increasing numbers of people to seek refuge in fundamentalist creeds and chants. The Bomb lurks somewhere along the borders of consciousness. Old values erode in a period of swift and bewildering change before new ones take their place. Small wonder that many wish to be left alone in the company of true believers under disciplines that require no effort of thought on their part. The right to be left alone, however, must have limits. The laws that protect human rights, including freedom from exploitation and undue influence, must apply evenly, in and out of sects, to everyone.

I was good the whole time, Legs. I upbraided no one, though I was heard to observe, on a late panel, that churches using the public air-waves to raise money should be glad to open their books to donors and revenuers. This proved to be too much for one delegate, a little cut by that time, who allowed that if this was what British Canadians thought, the Boston Tea Party had been a success. Mildly I rejoined, "What's so great about secrecy?" I am learning to turn the other cheek.

Nor did I let on that there was another religion more to my liking: the indolent, self-forgetful scepticism that never strung anyone up or whipped a child. I figured that this was neither the time nor the place for anything like that.

No, Legs, I was not, in spite of my innate modesty and forbearance, a model delegate at that conference. For I did not carry away the message that had been gift wrapped for the delegates. Instead I was convinced that courts, in the protection of religious freedom, should stop where the money-making begins. That will be important in Canada now that religious freedom has become part of our Constitution. I hope the judges who climb the bench to interpret this, and other rights, will first breakfast well. Freedoms are never absolute and the courts should serve them up, like Goldilock's porridge, neither too hot nor too cold.

Weighty groups in Canada are now pressing harder than ever to have courts and Constitution protect what is called economic freedom, that is, rights of property, the right of money to breed money, of wealth to wield power and influence with the fewest of laws either to observe or break. I'm reminded of Mark McGuigan's campaign slogan that fell flat when he was seeking the Liberal leadership: The state has no place in the board rooms of the nation.

Socialists are more at home defining limits of economic freedom, or freedom of greed. There's lots of it in Los Angeles, making the place a Purgatory for the Poor and a Paradise for the Rich.

Oh, Economic Freedom, what crimes have been committed in thy Name! Economic freedom murdered electric rail transit in Los Angeles, in Vancouver and in most of the cities of North America. In Vancouver on Frances Street in the East End you can still see traces of the *corpus delicti* where the street car tracks used to run. In the days of my youth I could travel on those tracks all the way into hilly downtown New Westminster for a (post-puberty) fare of 14 cents and to far-away Chilliwack for a few cents more.

In Los Angeles my wife and I toured the Scene of the Crime in a rented car. We sped along the freeways, shake, rattle and roll, alongside macho boys of all ages in half-tons, safaris and hearses, hurtling through a miasma of dioxides and toxcins, burning up rubber and metal and oil, like so many damned souls out on day parole. One commuter, I was told, was seen to smile in the morning rush traffic. The patrol pulled him over.

The Crime has been documented in the case of Los Angeles, not yet in Vancouver's case. There was a Conspiracy, and no doubt about it, by General Motors, Firestone Rubber and Standard Oil, to do rail transit in. The Companies even suffered a conviction for it in Chicago and were fined $5,000 a piece! They simply wanted to sell more cars, rubber and gas. So they clandestinely formed front companies to buy up street cars and tracks. Hundreds of miles of track disappeared from Los Angeles around 1950. The Companies wreaked more damage upon the cities than Attila the Hun did on Rome. And, with the help of their hired flacks and smoke-and-mirror men, they made the commuters like it. They made the consumers forget the toll of dead and wounded on the pavements, the mephitic air, the concrete spaghetti intersections, the stacked parking lots and the bumper-to-bumper time lost.

What am I saying? Made the consumer forget? Does not economic freedom enthrone the Consumer as King with the power to summon industry to lay before his feet the goods and services he wants at competitive prices? Well, yes, part of that is true, and that part should be preserved. Consumer choice does splay our shelves and storerooms with an array of products as rich as in an Aladdin's Cave. And yet, and yet, is there really an informed consumer who knows what he wants, with the ability to dictate to industry? Or a consumer too often manipulated by the hidden hand of money?

I think that I shall never see, lightbulbs that outlast me or thee. Bad that would be for business. And perhaps never see simple comparative information about life insurance put out by an impartial Consumers' Affairs Branch. Still it's the larger deflection of the economy away from any sensible respect for the public interest that really gets me down. Ask your father-in-law, a distinguished doctor, about the influence of money in warping our priorities through the promotion of nicotine products. Ask about the costs in sooty lungs, faint hearts, hospital beds, bereavements. Not that I'd draw a line and prohibit smoking. Instead I'd undercut the financial interests of tobacco companies (and farmers) that contribute so much to the social cost. I'd do in the common good what

American Tobacco and friends do against it.

I pause to relight my cigar.

Yes, dollars deflect the economy, and minds. You have heard me say, Legs, that generations of children's minds have been rinsed and bleached as they sat for hours in front of their TV sets. Conversation and the delights of reading were equally lost on these lost generations. Here I know I am getting into deep waters. For children, of all ages, *want* the baby formula that constitutes most North American television programming. They want it almost as much as the TV companies and their clever advertisers want to give it to them. Who am I to dictate to parents or adults, or to suggest that we close off the skies to give people only what I think is good for them? That solution is worse than the problem. Anyway science is rapidly making it difficult even for dictators to stop people from seeing and hearing whatever they want (right on!), what with pocket-sized cassettes, easily recopied tapes, and TV signals bouncing off satellites. The only solution is to put sufficient resources into good programming so that it's attractive enough to drive out the bad. What if better programming makes people shift their mental gears? No one ever died of that! I'll bet in time they'll like it better than the *Star Wars* that uses only the first ten years of their brains. We've got to find the money to buy Hamlet a new suit of clothes, and rent an old castle for a backdrop, so folks will be glad to see him in their homes. We've also got to give community TV outlets the resources to enable them to pull viewers away from the big American networks.

And before I leave consumer choice, which has such a fine democratic ring to it, let me remind you that in the market place it is not one consumer one vote; it's one dollar one vote. How does that distort, let's say, our housing priorities? The last time I was in California I dropped into some of the sumptuous holiday condominiums of Canadians in the Sun Belt. Some had more gold-

filigreed bathrooms that I or anyone else had the kidney
for. In Canada, many line up in dark halls to use one. The
needs of the poor wait upon the wants of the rich.

As I said, some hefty groups in the name of economic
freedom are trying to slip the words "property rights" into
the Canadian Charter. They are within a whisker of doing
it. How easily they beguile the public with their slogans:
"A Man's Home is his Castle," "Stop Big Government,"
"Do what you like with your Own." Beware, Legs!
Entrenching property rights in the Constitution would put
democratic Parliaments even more at the mercy of lawyers
and courts than they are today, with worse results than
ever for the chronically sub-rich.

How he worried about the interests of the propertied
classes in a democracy, that Father of Confederation, Sir
John A. Macdonald. I was named after him (quite a long
time after) and we share a Celtic, if not bibulous, nose,
though he is not a lineal ancestor. Sir John A. inserted an
appointed Senate into our BNA Act, believing that such a
Chamber of sometimes sober second thought could be
counted upon to uphold the rights of property. Otherwise,
he fretted, the many poor would vote to help themselves to
the money of the wealthy few. He needn't have bothered
his head. Canadian governments and courts have treated
property interests with tender, loving care, while the
Senate and its veto have peacefully snored.

We had a fine object lesson of that in 1961 in British
Columbia. Premier W.A.C. Bennett, in a fit of lucidity,
called a summer Session of the Legislature to bring the
B.C. Electric Company under public ownership. The
shareholders had him in court the next day and before the
legal system let go of him, the people had to pay the
shareholders another $25 million—and pay legal fees all
around. So tell me, please, why should we, the Reds, want
to strew more legal obstacles in our path?

Yet some of us apparently do, for in September, 1982,

our MLAs in a fit of lunacy supported a formal Socred resolution to insert property rights into the Charter. An election was in the offing, and the Socreds wanted to put the NDP on the spot by making us vote as if we did not believe in the sacred rights of private ownership. They fully expected us to oppose their resolution, with good reason, for in Ottawa Ed Broadbent had already expressed his opposition.

What a bad day we had. Our Caucus had ten minutes to discuss this resolution before tumbling into our seats in the Legislature without having reached a decision. There instead of adjourning the debate, some of our speakers said the resolution was just a Socred political ploy and that property rights were Motherhood and everyone knows we're for that. I got a hot collar and took off—abstained. I should have raised hell but loyalty to colleagues and Party, just before an election, made a coward of me.

You'd be surprised to know how much property rights take in. Lawyers define property as anything a person has dominion over. Years ago the American courts declared that child labour laws were out of bounds because the factory owner's property rights would be impaired if he was not allowed to employ twelve-year-old children. Not that our courts will ever go that far but the example shows the width of the discretion that the courts would have. No way should rights that primarily benefit the well-off get into the Charter. One person's right to own makes it harder for the dispossessed to enjoy the same right.

I myself, Legs, this fat cat, have property rights to the edge of the sea, which stand in the way of the full use of the beach by the public. I refer to my "riparian" rights between the foreshore and my home on English Bay (where I've often asked you to drop in). Some day the City of Vancouver will at last get around to putting a public park and walk-way right on top of those riparian rights of mine. When it does, should I, or should I not, have a

Constitutional Right's case to block those public plans or at least to make the city pay me more money before they can go ahead?

You know, Legs, property includes not only Incorporeal Hereditaments (disembodied whats?) but also seniority rights under union agreements. They're good rights. They protect, say, the older worker from being fired to make way for a young fellow with more hustle. Today, however, only a minority of workers have this protection, and even in happier days to come, some will still have more of it than others. They will always give, for instance, Smith, who's been longer on the job, a better chance for a promotion than Jones. And they will always involve competing social interests; in one corner the advantages of seniority protection; in the other corner the claims of hard work and talent to make their way up in the world to the general advantage of all. Seniority is a private, contractual right and shouldn't be enshrined in the Charter along with basic civil liberties equally applicable to all.

The ordinary union member keeps his seniority subject to an Arbitration Board's review of his performance and any misconduct. Seniority goes by the name of "tenure" in the Elysium Fields of Academia. Tenure gives illustrations of how this right—good in allowing professors to express unpopular opinion—can be carried too far. Only one Professor has lost his tenure in the 73-year history of UBC. And he still kept hold of it after being convicted on two counts of theft of university money. Only later did he lose it (after much public outrage) for issuing a misleading press release! What politician has not done that?

Yes, there can also be cases where the rights of tenure conflict with the rights of lowly students to a good education. A university instructor may give out the same old stuff year after year in a nine- or twelve-hour teaching week and close his office door at three o'clock to students seeking extra help. Don't tell me that behind the Veil of Academic Freedom there aren't hidden abuses, as well as meritorious dedication and ability.

What then of the right to strike, to quit work collectively to try to get better conditions? Should this right be in the Constitution? I'd prefer not (though see below). It would increasingly draw the courts into making decisions that are essentially economic and social, and into weighing the competing claims of various groups. What one group wins another may lose, and losers can be other trade unionists or plain consumers, and not just big corporations or governments who can pass the costs along.

However, the courts are getting into this field, and, that being so, I agree with the recent decision of the Ontario Divisional Court. It held that the words "freedom of association" in the Charter included "the freedom to organize, to bargain collectively and, as a necessary corollary, to strike." At the same time, that case, while allowing public employees to strike, held they were nonetheless bound by what the Court considered to be reasonable wage guidelines. In effect the Court held that Legislatures, subject to the courts, can impose limits on what can be struck for. To unionists this will look like a case of "yes, you can go swimming, my darling daughter, hang your clothes on a hickory limb, but don't go near the water." Did the Court contradict itself, Legs? In a way, but life itself throws up contradictions.

Incidentally, do the words "freedom of association" imply also a freedom to dissociate? There'll be cases coming down the pike, Legs, arguing that the right to belong to a union includes the right not to, and what does that do to the union shop? It really makes you think that we were better off when courts were not involved in these questions, and hope that they will have the good sense to limit the extent of their involvement.

Indubitably, though, the courts should zealously defend

personal dignity against discrimination because of race, creed or gender. The sad death in December of my friend Quon Wong reminds me of what he did to advance the cause of freedom from discrimination, a freedom which didn't exist in this province when he was growing up. Quon was my friend of 40 years; more than a friend, my genial mentor of common sense and manners. When he came here from China as a youngster our Chinese community was denied every civil right. The Chinese who laid the CPR tracks through the Rocky Mountains could not bring their wives or children to join them in Canada. Later they became market gardeners and houseboys, obsequious as a condition of survival.

In 1951 I had lunch with Quon on Pender Street. Oriental Canadians had at last been given the right to vote (Native Indians, too). The unintended result was that Quon as a registered voter was entitled to apply to become a Notary Public. Together we prepared affidavits of fitness and need and appeared before one Justice Coady in Supreme Court Chambers. (Showing good taste all around, you married his granddaughter.)

In those days applications for a notarial seal were not supposed to reach the court at all without first being passed upon by the back-room boys who controlled patronage. Justice Coady ignored that practice. He, too, was eager to end the long night of discrimination. On May 15, 1951, he made Quon a Notary without further ado, the first Chinese in Canada to enter a legal profession. Years later, as Attorney-General, I made Quon's nephew a Judge, again a first in Canada, with no qualms that I was benefiting a relative of my friend.

Now, thankfully, the Charter with the simple words "everyone is equal under the law" has officially ended racial discrimination, and curtailed most discriminatory conduct. Most but not all, for the law cannot extirpate dislikes, and prejudice will out. Prejudice comes in part from ignorance about other people and their lives; mainly it springs from poverty and unfairness. Deprivations engender resentments and undermine the sense of community. Good economics can do more for good civilities than any laws, though both are necessary.

Voting is an obvious way for prejudice by the majority to express itself against minorities, and the law can't do anything about that. Politicians rarely know what voters really think. The only times voters have let slip to me that they'd never support an Asiatic, or how darker skins were ruining their neighbourhoods, were occasions when a white NDP candidate was running against someone of Chinese or Sikh ancestry. Those Philistines are, I think, relatively few in the United Nations of peoples that Vancouver East has become. I've seen the riding change from what was an electorate of mainly British stock through successive waves of newcomers—Italian, Slavic, Chinese, Portuguese, Punjabi. New Canadians move east from the city core as they can afford to buy a house, and some later move on to the suburbs as they become more prosperous. For a while new arrivals encounter subterranean intolerance but usually this gives way to good neighbourliness and mutual assistance among varied families in the same block.

That's how I have seen it. Lately, however, I have been picking up more signs of intolerance. A teacher tells me she had to break up a fight on the school grounds between rival students of different races. A couple complains that when they apply, the "room to let" sign comes down and they are met with "it's been taken." Nevertheless, I'm basically hopeful. I look ahead to my grandchildren growing up harmoniously in a country as rich in the diversity of its races, creeds and cultures as any place on earth. Who would want to live in a homogenized society? Not I. A Roman long ago praised the beauty of diversity in the words, "Diversitas fecit pulchrum." One day there'll be a Canada, Legs, without intolerance, where opportunities abound, with a Canadian Irishman saying, "In this country one man's as good as another, and, for the matter of that, often a good deal better."

It will take moxie to give prejudice a decent burial. We have to recognize, for one thing, that there is a point where the application of laws against discrimination becomes counter-productive. Courts and Human Rights Tribunals have to proceed with care and restraint. The object is not to find some bigot and make him boiling mad. The object is to raise the level of mutual respect for differences in the reservoir.

Human Rights Codes should be evenly enforced in large institutions but not necessarily in small. A while ago I gave some legal advice to a young Sikh friend who, after losing his job, started a small trucking business with an uncertain competitive future. Suppose he gives some preference in hiring to Sikhs looking for work. Should an investigator be assigned to that case? Or suppose a Jewish businessman is more likely to employ Jewish secretaries, or Chinese restauranteurs to employ Chinese waiters (not, heaven forbid, Scottish. Scottish!). I wouldn't want some tribunal to characterize too many natural human inclinations as offences under the law. Take another area. We do need laws against the inculcation of racial hatred against an ethnic minority. But an Attorney-General should think carefully before a charge is laid. He should not give, say, a neo-Nazi a courtroom to use as a national platform to clear and present danger of injury to a group.

There's nothing wrong, Legs, in a court or commission using quotas, on the right occasions, to rectify discrimination or to give a helping hand to a disadvantaged group. I did it once, as Attorney-General, by setting aside some places in the law school for Native Indian students. Some argue that this kind of action amounts to discrimination in itself against non-Indian students competing for admissions. However, I don't see it as a denial of the "legal" rights of such students. They have no more "right" to be admitted regardless of race than they have to be considered regardless of where they live. This was an instance where special help to a disadvantaged minority outweighed other private interests.

Would I now favour a quota of places in the law school for women students? Undoubtedly there are cases where women should have special help because of the handicaps they have faced from traditions of male supremacy, if not downright prejudice. Still, in law school admissions, departures from the test of excellence should be rare. Increasing numbers of excellent Portias are making it into the law on their own. The real problem is the financial barriers which prevent, perhaps more women students than men, from meeting the costs of legal training, and these should be lowered to widen opportunities.

About the same time, I was able to widen opportunities for women by repealing a regulation which was an obnoxious example of prejudice. A modest assault on patriarchy! The regulation decreed that "no woman can serve liquor in a bar or lounge." Tavern keepers protested against the repeal as did the male waiters. The latter claimed to be incensed on high moral grounds, holding that women, the poor things, could become depraved in those dens of iniquity. Nonsense. It was the jobs and the money they were thinking of, and money is one of the roots of prejudice.

But no quotas, please, Legs, when it comes to elections! Our last convention in Regina amended the constitution to give women half the places on the elected National Executive. Really! Grace MacInnis, our fighting game hen, used to ask election meetings to support what she stood for, and *not* vote for her because she was a woman. I am afraid that convention bestowed a badge of inferiority upon the women delegates, though many did not think so.

Affirmative action, and equal pay for work of equal value, are useful expedients in particular situations to rectify discrimination. Never forget, however, that these expedients, though an excellent avenue, are a poor second to widening opportunities all round, and to lessening income disparities all round.

Are you still with me, Legs? Am I muddling you up? Well, let me try listing the major civil rights that we count upon the courts to protect and advance. There are critics on the far-left who claim that our vaunted civil liberties are meaningless to those without enough money to make use of them. Whatever truth there is to their claim does not add up to a justification for abandoning any liberties.

Freedom of Speech—the rights to know, to utter and to argue, inherited from the English Common Law—will always be the chief ornament of civilized society. Around us today is an abundance of ideas to read and think and speak about. The spreading chestnut tree of free expression has been nurtured by the ideals of forebears as diverse as Erasmus, John Milton and Mary Wollstone-craft. The trick for socialists is to enlarge the opportunities for people to exercise free expression on a more equal basis without diminishing by a jot that hard won legal right.

Obviously, some with money to burn have more of this equal right than others; if you don't believe me ask Free Speech's rich uncle, Free Press. Those who own a TV station or sit on the board of a newspaper chain exert subtle and not-so-subtle influences upon public opinion. How can we make the media more responsive to the discussion and presentation of things that really matter for ordinary people? State control is out of the question, although I don't rule out press councils of wise old owls to set right citizens' complaints. Mainly I look to stronger editorial trade unions to impose journalistic integrity upon news managements that cut, suppress or distort, along with more community ownership of news outlets.

There is one area in which all our prized rights of free expression seem powerless to control events. The North American military-industrial complex goes its way virtually unchecked by public opinion. It has as its command the power to inculcate fears to justify new weapons systems; to let contracts to suppliers who often have interests in radio, television and newspapers; to purchase politicians who want military dollars spent in their constituencies; and to direct university research teams with military grants. This unchecked power can blow us all to smithereens and in my bad moments I think that the west is becoming a mirror image of Russian news management under which military demands, class privileges and corruption alike escape the scrutiny of public opinion.

At least on this side we have legal rights to impart information, with few limits placed upon those rights by the courts. One limit protects others from defamation; one, while allowing you to criticize a judicial decision, prevents you from talking back to the Judge. Which reminds me, Legs, though it shouldn't, of one accused who was asked if he had anything to say before sentence was passed upon him. Highly incensed by his conviction, the accused replied to the Judge, who was fortunately hard of hearing, "Nothing, you bastard." Cupping his ear, the Judge asked his clerk, "What did he say?" "Nothing, you bastard," said the clerk, whereupon the Judge rejoined, "That's funny, I thought I saw his lips move."

Treat the courts with respect, Legs, and they will, I think, protect your right to be unpopular and feel safe about it. I have a feeling I'm in training to become unpopular in my latter days, no mean feat for a lifelong politician!

Equality before the Law—"The Law in its majestic equality," wrote Anatole France, "forbids rich as well as poor from sleeping under bridges, begging in the streets or stealing bread." These words came back to me when I was in London and watched some elderly men spreading cardboard from old cartons to make their beds on the grass in Lincoln's Fields. One hundred yards away Judges of the High Court were also retiring in their diggings in Lincoln's Inn. The repose of each was protected in equal measure by the Common Law of England, though they were not about to change places. An abyss separated their social lots.

Strange, Legs, we pride ourselves on giving everyone a fair trial in the courts while many are condemned to death in the market place: small farmers wiped out by a freak of nature; the emotionally disturbed and those who have caught the disease of alcoholism; still others tossed on the scrap heap of unemployment. What due process have these had?

And, even for those well-enough off, how prohibitive is the cost of access to justice? A Vietnamese boat-person, later an engineer, came to my office, too late for much good I could do him. He had contested with his wife custody of their infant child and the amount of any child maintenance. His lawyer was a "specialist" in domestic relations. He and his wife went through a sixteen-day trial in the Supreme Court. When I saw him, his own legal bill was $45,000 and his specialist was launching an appeal. There was never any reason to deny his wife custody, and no court was going to give it to him anyway for he was something of a martinet. It reminds me of Voltaire, who wrote that he had only been ruined twice—once when he lost a law suit and once when he won one.

The law is no exception to the rule that establishments grow by what they feed on. Reform and simplification has to be a continual process, but how hard it is. There's a Trial Lawyers' Association that is vociferous in its opposition to the no-fault compensation of the victims of automobile accidents. No-fault would take these damage claims out of the courts, for the most part, patch up all of the victims, and visit penalties in fines and demerit points on those guilty of safety infractions. The trial lawyers oppose this in the name of Magna Carta, not, of course, in the name of their fees that run from 30 to 40 per cent of awards. This association used to hold an annual banquet to fete the Judge of the Year, presumably for the size of his awards, until the Bench scotched that. (Do some of those lawyers, by the way, consider advertising and price competition a clear breach of legal ethics?)

Don't get me wrong. The right to a day in court, or to an open, impartial tribunal, is a pillar of liberties. The courts are also solvents of the resentments generated in disputes between citizens or between citizens and the state. I recall (here I go again!) my client of years ago, Andy Good, a lumber sawyer who was the portly, drawling, spitting image of Andy Devine, the comic. My Andy was charged with impaired driving after wheeling his old car right up to the counter of the drugstore that used to stand at 4th and Burrard. He came to a halt in a hailstorm of broken glass and flying boxes. He should have been charged with breaking and entering. At his trial, assisted by the testimony of a drinking buddy, who conveniently was a mechanic, Andy explained how he had been overcome by carbon monoxide fumes from a leaky exhaust pipe. The Judge was so astonished by this incredible story that he acquitted Andy on the spot. My client turned to me, sorry that the pantomime was over, and asked, "Is there anything else?" "Yes, Andy," I replied, "here is my bill."

The Right to Silence—the mirror image of free speech, I suppose, is free silence. Criminal lawyers, all lawyers for that matter, assure me that the right not to incriminate one's self is a hallmark of our freedoms. Is it now? What's coming over me? I look like a lawyer, walk and even talk like one, but in my sunset years I'm starting not to think like one.

What's so bad about someone in some circumstances

being called upon to account for his or her conduct? A crime lord to account for his ill-gotten wealth? The husband (with mistress) of a poisoned wife to explain the weed killer in the garage? I don't want confessions elicited by a detective's trick questions or extorted in a jail with the help of a rubber truncheon. I'm talking about fessing up in open court to whatever you know about something serious that has happened in which you were involved.

The rape victim scours the police line-up in search of her assailant, who had worn a stocking mask during the crime. He, on the best legal advice, has nothing to say about the night in question. Only simple souls incriminate themselves, like the drunk stockbroker in the line-up, who blurted out, "That's the girl." (That joke, Legs, has been run through the Macdonald De-Ethnification Purifier.)

The Swiss criminal justice system does not detract from general liberties. There, an accused charged with a serious offence, when evidence points in his or her direction, is subject to cross-examination by a Judge. That does not convict the innocent, though fewer of the guilty walk away. It does mean that trials are shorter and less expensive than the marathon proceedings we see in our courts. And it would, I think, mean a safer community.

Without continual reform, justice can be lost in the interstices of criminal procedures. Often, too often, the prosecution, in order to convict anyone, grants immunity and cash and a hideaway to one of the accused who can be persuaded to turn on his pals and give state's evidence. That's hardly an equal application of the laws. Pre-trial examinations might not stop this practice, but would certainly make it less necessary.

Still we go on, enamoured of the old ways, with some benefiting from them. Now the Charter gives juveniles charged with indictable offenses the right to a lawyer, whose first advice to a guilty youngster will be to say nothing. The principle that the Crown must prove everything beyond a reasonable doubt collides with the social interest in preventing house break-ins and rehabilitating young offenders. Confession, they say, is good for the soul. Would it not be equally good for a young person to own up to the damage he has done to someone else? You know, Legs, after the initial shock, some youngsters, acting up and out, begin to enjoy playing the legal game in the courts. Retribution, by no means condign, but swift and certain, is the best and only mender of wayward dispositions.

Where should the line be drawn between one person's right to keep personal information confidential and the rights of others to know? I confess I've always been for giving a lot of scope to the right to know. To my mind, people shouldn't get upset because their Social Security number is public knowledge or even their medical history. In any case, as a practical matter, it's becoming almost impossible to keep such things secret. We're into an age awash with information—surveillance cameras watch cash transactions, data banks store multitudinous facts. Countless persons have access to records; and snoops, perhaps with a little money under the table, can get at them by hook or by crook. And the more that's open, the likelier are gossips to tell the truth.

There are some clear cases where rights of privacy bump into rights to know. Why shouldn't public records be open to track down a husband on the lam after deserting his wife and the children? Or UIC records be open to help locate missing persons? I'd even have some well-known military secrets out in the open even if that leads some spies into early retirement.

What do you think, Legs? Should a candidate be able to keep his history of mental illness in the dark until elected to Parliament where it won't be noticed? Should a candidate who had a criminal record as a youth not have to run on it? I believe that the voters would prefer a candidate who has rehabilitated himself over one they don't really feel they know.

Some civil libertarians say that we shouldn't take the fingerprints of a juvenile to compare them with those on a stolen car, and that the record should certainly be destroyed if prints are taken. But if police officers have the prints on file might that not help to discourage some youngster from following a light-fingered career?

It's a free and tolerant society, not a secretive one, that fosters human eccentricities. Secrecy is the hallmark of totalitarian regimes.

On the other hand, surveillance, search warrants, telephone taps and so on, should be employed only where they are justified by good social reasons. At our Boag Conference last November, which brought together many of the leading democratic socialist thinkers from around the world, a delegate quite rightly complained about the tyranny of electronic surveillance and work measurement at the job site. Abuses of that kind can and must be checked by the terms of union agreements or by legislation or both. But then she got carried away! She went on to complain that it was getting harder all the time to lie a little at the border when Customs Officers had pictures of you and your car. I tried to assure her that there would always be places where the ancient arts of lying could be practised. Not in the courts, of course, but in other places, perhaps even in Legislatures; and certainly during the rites of courtship!

> *When my love swears that she is made of truth*
> *I do believe her though I know she lies*

What a fetish we make about the confidentiality of Income Tax Returns. Not that ordinary people should care. Everyone at work knows (or should know) what fellow workers make. But the scions of inherited wealth care—and benefit from the secrecy; tax cheaters care. Mr. Big, who finances the drug deals without coming close to the white stuff, cares. It's his couriers, desperate to make $1,500 on a return trip to Hong Kong, who serve the time in jail. A lawyer says that tax information can benefit someone's competitors or queer a deal. I think business activity will go just as well when all the facts are in the open.

They weren't with it, or were they, those old boys who put into the Regina Manifesto that "full publicity must be given to Income Tax payments." They wanted the disparities out in full view. Oh, how offensive to capitalistic proprieties that would be!

It's time to say good-bye, Legs. I'm beginning to get bunions on my cerebral lobes. All NDPers are agreed upon maximizing everyone's liberties in ways compatible with the liberties of all others, although we may not agree on priorities. Some say that one individual's freedom ends where another's begins. It's not as easy as that. What is certain is that freedoms can't be bargained away for the sake of economic justice or efficiency; that's what divides us from the Communists.

In Berlin last year, with the Wall staring at me, it was easy to know what should be inalienable. To speak freely, criticize, associate, elect, travel, know. Beside me someone asked what those things meant to someone without a job or reduced to destitution. He said that on the other side of the Wall the word "Arbeitslossen," meaning unemployment, was unknown, however familiar it was in West Germany.

Yes, our commitment to civic freedoms must rest upon a broader commitment to human values, one which ensures that freedoms will not be eroded by economic injustice in the midst of potential plenty. Those civic

freedoms, nevertheless, are non-negotiable.
Not an easy path we've chosen, Legs. But our own.

Yours for Liberty, etc.,

Alex

'FREE ENTERPRISE DOES NOT, OF COURSE, MEAN SILLY COMPETITION'

Vancouver General Hospital
Vancouver, B.C.
January 31, 1984

My dear Legs,

This time I'm flat on my back in VGH. I have a tube in my left nostril, a pencil in one hand, no cigar in the other and am being pumped and irrigated like a farmer's field. My burst appendix was caused, I think, by a bout of boredom during my holiday in the sun belt. I was born at an early age on the second (or seventh) floor of this hospital and now I'm on the tenth, getting up there. When I came to from the anesthetic, there were nurses and flowers all around me and I thought I must have died and gone to the Senate. Today my surgeon, who was a real virtuoso, said he'd release me in a few days but insisted that I'd still be under the nurse. And, he added, no chasing your rumble seat around a squash court for at least six weeks.

Jimmy Rhodes was in and brought me a posy. He talked of the good old days of the NDP Government when I was Energy Minister as well as A.G. I had made Jimmy head of our B.C. Petroleum Corporation and he promptly made me the scourge of the Gas and Oil men. His visit gave me the idea of writing to you about energy. Writing about energy in my present state is akin to psychiatrists giving helpful advice to people who are happier than they are.

He reminisced about how, in 1973, we had broken an honest-to-God contract under which our natural gas had been going over the border for a ridiculously low price and how we had confused Wall Street by socializing the gas instead of the oil wells. To do this, we had to finagle our way around some pretty tough hombres, including Kelly Gibson, Head of the gas carrier West Coast Transmission. Kelly was a shrewd Oklahoman who kept one eye on the Bible and the other on his till. One morning he had me reciting verses from Deuteronomy to a Prayer Breakfast of businessmen, every one of whom had been saved. He loved to try out his line on us in mournful tones: "I hope we break even this year. We can *sure* use the money." I told Jimmy the hose down my nose only hurt when I laughed.

We had jumped at the chance to socialize natural gas. British Columbia has been gift wrapping its resource rights for the international companies ever since it became a province. And once a province or a country parts with the equity in its resources, getting it back is no easy matter, and the companies who get the resource rights can find ways of getting the resources across the line to their parent companies at bargain prices.

It's a game of monopoly, Legs, and B.C. is the board. The players come from all over but mostly from the USA. They know every trick of the game. One gets timber cutting rights, another mineral claims, others coal licences, gas permits, oil leases, grazing rights and even exclusive privileges to shoot animals. All of these are hot items to sell or trade on the speculative exchanges. B.C.'s just lucky to be still holding its water. And when the natives complain, they are told that they still own the board, so don't cry.

The NDP says that alienation of resource rights has to stop, without, however, really knowing what to do about the rights that have already fallen into the hands of the international mega-corporations. Should we sit down with them and plan joint public-private ventures? Yes, if they'll let us. Should we buy as many of their shares as we can? That is a very costly proposition. Should we control them? Shoot, Legs, we're supposed to be controlling them now. Tell me, I pray, who is the ventriloquist and who is the dummy? Eric Kierans, a Red Liberal and Cabinet Minister, later a President of the Montreal Stock Exchange until they found a heart in him, delivered himself of the following:

"Governments no longer control companies, companies control governments. A company like Inco comes into Sudbury, Ontario, and takes out millions of dollars in profit, which it invests in Guatemala. Then it cuts back in Sudbury and throws Canadians out of work. When the government makes a little noise, Inco says, 'If you interfere with us, we may have to reduce our production even more.' "

So, it comes down to public ownership of at least parts of the operation of the multinational companies (or does it, Legs?). Well, it happens that with each new manifesto the NDP prints, "public ownership" has been slipping down into the fine print or has become just a footnote. It's losing support even among our foot soldiers, as if it were a penny stock slipping off the financial pages into the "Help Wanted" after the promoters have dumped their shares. For NDPers too can pick up some of the communicable diseases spread around by the ad men and big business. You know their lines: "big profits are good for you"; "the post office is less efficient than smoke signals"; workers will sit down if they're not already lying down, unless the shares of their companies are privately owned. And NDPers, myself included, worry about the public costs. Some wonder whether we can afford to buy our country back and others whether we can afford not to.

Oil, gas and coal—those fugacious black substances have been in and out of my life for many years. I am going to take you back in time with them, Legs, because unless we know the past we can't understand the present or make the kind of future we want. I could have made wood or nickel or iron my example, the plot line of one or the other doesn't differ that much. I just happen to know more about the fossil substances.

In 1934, my father, Mr. Justice M.A. Macdonald (known to his friends as M.A.), was appointed by his friend Duff Patullo, the Liberal Premier, sole Commissioner to investigate B.C.'s oil and coal industries. M.A. had once served a Liberal administration as A.G. (that job was out of our family for 54 years until I was sworn back into it) and later M.A. became Chief Justice of the Province. I had myself been a Liberal until the age of 3. By 1934 I was in long pants and had become a book socialist. I used to bring home far-left tomes like John Strachey's *The Coming Struggle for Power* and leave them around the house for my father to pick up, hoping thereby to educate the old fellow in the facts of life.

In the early 30s oil was driving coal out of the industrial markets. Bustling mining communities were turning into ghost towns as the coal mines shut down and unemployed miners left to do road work in the relief camps for 25 cents a day. In the public outcry, the oil companies were charged with dumping their heavy fuel oil from California and Peru onto the B.C. market at less than the cost of bringing it in, with the result that boilers in saw mills, mines and railways were converting over from coal to oil. In short, the oil companies were charged with getting rid of their bunker oil, an otherwise unsalable by-product of their oil wells, while driving coal out of the rich industrial markets of the future. At the same time, so it was said, the oil companies made up their losses on bunker fuel by overcharging the man behind the steering wheel for his gasoline. After three arduous years, M.A. found the oil companies guilty as charged.

Pictures come back from those far off times—it's the years in between that slip from memory. One fine May morning my father was on the mark for a foray into enemy territory in California where the black oil was sucked from the ground. In the porte cochere of the big house in Shaughnessy Heights, he sat behind the wheel of his old touring Cadillac, top down, brightly buffed, a wicker picnic basket and thermos on the back seat. M.A. wore a baseball cap to break the wind, my mother sat behind him in a kerchief. The farewell guard of honour drawn up on the steps consisted of the children, the Chinese cook, the cocker spaniel, the gardener and his wife.

The oil companies had offered to finance the choicest hotel rooms and trimmings along the route but M.A. wouldn't take a nickel from the subjects of his investigation. (Today politicians and officials feel slighted if their influence is not recognized by drinks and hot meals.) The proferred perks by no means indicated that the companies were pleased by this mission; quite the contrary. They didn't like anyone poking around in their books, and, indeed, checking their arithmetic was not easy. For the majority were integrated companies, vertically, horizontally, every which way. They had it all, from the oil rigs to the service pumps. They could come up with a loss in any part of the system as easily as a profit. Already they had the swagger of the newly rich, confident that they were on their way to a position of power, privilege and pelf unparalleled in history.

Simple souls wondered, even in those days, how it came to be that the posted tank wagon price for a gallon of gasoline was the same in any town for each of the companies. It was a case of "After You, Alphonse." They took turns. When its turn came, Imperial would quote the price and the others, by an odd coincidence, followed suit after a decent interval, so odd that it moved a Montrealer, John D. Ketchum, to rhapsodize:

> *Free enterprise does not of course mean silly competition,*
> *And cutting prices is a sin for which there's no remission;*
> *Oh, a Gentleman's agreement is the best of all devices,*
> *To stabilize our Dividends, our Profits and our Prices.*

Mind you, the companies did compete in sales, and advertised the unique qualities of the gas they sold, even if came out of the other fellow's tanks. Competition in prices was, however, in their view carrying the principle of Free Enterprise a step too far. So unseemly it would have been to cut each other's throat. Well, may you ask, Legs, why no prosecutor has ever taken the oil companies to court under the Combines Act. There are two answers. You can guess the first; the second is that it's pretty hard to prosecute a pressed hand or a wink and a nod in the sanctuary of the Albany Club in Toronto.

M.A.'s report in three volumes was published on December 5, 1938. It was an eye opener. The oil companies had indeed sold "heavy fuel oil in the Province below costs," the report said, "in order to unfairly drive coal from the market place." The report also found "that gasoline could be sold at a fair profit at eighteen cents a gallon. Or, if the public wanted to tolerate the present inefficient distribution system designed to maintain prices and prevent competition, it could be sold for 23 cents a gallon."

The report was seen as heresy by the companies and, like the Albigensian heresy, had to be stamped out. New Jersey might hear, it could be catching. In Duff Patullo, however, they encountered a doughty fighter. Duff was the kind of Liberal like my father and Eric Kierans who go the wrong way down a one way street of life, becoming more radical with the years. Duff summoned the Legislature and set up a Petroleum Board that promptly ordered a three cent cut in the price of gasoline.

"Confiscatory!" cried the companies on the way to the court house. Their lawyer was the influential Senator John Wallace de Beque Farris, who made judges and then appeared in their courts where they found him quite convincing. This is perhaps an instance of the old saw that it is better to know the judge than to know the law.

When the case reached the Court of Appeal, my father could not sit in judgment on his own report. Still, Legs, if you read the judgment in the case (Home Oil versus A.G. of B.C., 1940), you will find a long judgment by an Appeal Judge who usually, whatever the case, said no more than "I dissent" or "I agree with my brethren." I naughtily suspect that my father wrote that judgment and his laconic colleague signed it.

Foiled in the courts, the companies resorted to discipline. They knew how to discipline a competitor. Now it was to be a province. They went on strike—a strike of capital against government. It was not the usual sort of strike with pickets and scuffles breaking out and wives skimping to make do without a pay cheque. Instead, service station attendants waited for tank wagon trucks that never came. Lickerish swains really ran out of gas in Stanley Park. Cars were stranded on bridges and trestles, with the police ticketing them and towing them away. Desperate gas junkies organized treks across the border to fill their tanks.

Finally the government sought a truce. The three-cent reduction was reduced to two cents. The companies accepted, biding their time, still determined to do Duff in. They knew how to mix oil and politics. Their chance came in 1945. Those Liberals and Conservatives who the companies could work with got together to form a Coalition to beat the CCF (sound familiar?). Everyone knew Duff would have no part of it. "After all these years," he declared, "I am not going to get in bed with my political enemies." Soon he was to have no bed at all.

In 1948, the Petroleum Board offered the companies a three-cent increase. Not enough, they exclaimed, rattling their tin cups. Again, they went on strike. Shell tearfully announced that "further investment in this Province would have to be curtailed." Imperial cut its deliveries by 45 per cent. Pusillanimous Members of the Legislature quickly voted the Petroleum Board out of existence. The oil companies had done everything to the B.C. Legislature except refine it.

Today relations between Big Oil and its B.C. dependency are excellent. Heretics like M.A. and Duff have departed the scene, and for that matter, I don't feel all that well myself. Most of the locals have no idea just how brutally they are being price-fixed and the rest have no idea what if anything they can do about it. Besides, Esso brings them Hockey Night in Canada (brutality of a different sort).

But were they right, M.A. and Duff? I call to the witness stand Robert J. Bertrand (a Q.C., like me). He was Director of the Combines Branch in Ottawa. His report of February 27, 1981, covers the fifteen years from 1958 to 1973. He solemnly deposes that in those years price fixing by the oil companies cost the Canadian people $12 billion. That's 12 *billion* with a gulp! And the rascal goes on. That 12 billion, he says, if not skimmed off, but invested, makes the real loss to Canadians the fine sum of 89 billion dollars, enough to get rid of the deficit and the excuse for making the poor more miserable.

How the companies did it, and do it, you ask, Legs? It's the old story of parent companies charging their corporate children in Canada above the world price for crude oil; fixing their own carrying charges because they own the pipelines; refineries selling for the same prices as their competitors; service stations being told what their prices should be.

All the while the companies assure us that they must sell today's gasoline and heating oil at the cost of replacing it tomorrow. If your corner grocer sold his rolled oats for tomorrow's price, he'd soon own a race horse.

Let me give you some travel advice, Legs. Buy American dollars for your Sun Belt holiday in November. Because in December the Canadian dollar falls sick. Last December it fell below 80 cents. For that's the month dutiful Canadian corporate children send Christmas dividends to their parents. Imperial Oil alone changes about 200 million Canadian dollars into George Washingtons. So watch your timing. And tell Canadians to remember that they have to sell a lot of resources over the border to balance their housekeeping accounts.

I make a speech in the Legislature without getting much attention except from Gulf Oil's Director of Corporate Affairs, who read it in Hansard. I had said that some of Gulf's surplus "mad money" went into a huge real estate project in La Prairie, across the St. Lawrence from Montreal. The Director wrote to buck me up by pointing out that Gulf still had enough dollars left over to drill for more oil in the Beaufort Sea. Comfort thyself, Legs, foreign investment in Canada keeps rising—with our money, yet!

The Sovereign State of Exxon is the plumpest, if not the comliest of Oil's Seven Sisters. Its revenues in 1982 were $103 billion. Set that beside the gross national product of mere nations, and Exxon takes in more than Saudi Arabia, but less than Switzerland. Among the 189 nations of the world, Exxon ranks nineteenth in gross revenues. Exxon's net after taxes—four to five billion dollars.

Wars are fought over oil. Hitler did not invade Russia to put his armies on manoeuvres. He wanted Russian oil. If there's a World War III, Legs, and it lasts long enough for someone to throw a uniform on you, you'll be fighting over oil. Not to worry about World War IV. If there is one, you and I will be isotopes locked in dubious battle on the Plains of Heaven.

The nurse has changed my dressing and my scar has drawn another rave review. I turn to a more ethereal substance, natural gas. Duff was convinced that a reservoir of oil and natural gas lay beneath the Peace River area. These riches, he declared, are "the people's heritage," not to be alienated to a "gasoline super-state." He imposed a ban on private oil and gas rights. He knew drilling was a costly gambling adventure. But if it paid off for companies why not for people? He tried. In 1921, as Minister of Lands, he had the government drill six shallow wells with the few dollars he could scrape together. In 1940, as Premier, he tried again, with no luck either time. If only B.C. had persevered with oil and gas exploration as a public enterprise—but that's what might have been, Legs. What has been wasn't so nice. Duff's ban on private leases was lifted by the Coalition Government that dumped him.

First up to the counter was a syndicate put together by Frank McMahon. He was born poor in Moyie, B.C., became a roustabout in the Alberta oil fields, finally a stock promoter. He left that counter with Gas Permits Numbers 1, 2 and 3, covering 750,000 acres in the Peace. His syndicate included well-to-do Vancouver promoters, American petroleum and pipeline interests, and even Clint Murchison, the richest Texan oilman of them all.

They planned to pipe Peace natural gas down to Vancouver and over the border as far as San Francisco. Ottawa gave them an export permit, Victoria gave them a right of way for the pipeline and Washington, D.C., over the protests of other interests, gave them permission to service the American market. Their flagship was Westcoast Transmission Co. and they floated its shares amid eager anticipations.

But first the insiders gave themselves options to buy 625,000 shares at 5 cents each. Within three months these shares were quoted on the Stock Exchanges at $57! Without any risk (or tax at that time) the insiders made $35 million. Frank McMahon himself had about 150,000 of the 5 cent shares, 250,000 shares at $5, and 200,000 at $6. The roustabout had become a man of substance. And it was all as legal as it is illegal to steal a chicken.

Promoters' millions; who loses what the promoters gain? Elementary, my dear Legs. When a company issues cheap shares to insiders, instead of receiving fair value in a public share offering, the company loses and passes the loss on to consumers in higher prices. The public finally pays.

Frank McMahon also became a man of respectability. For in our venal culture, riches bring with them not only influence, but social standing. In 1958, frock-coated, he escorted Princess Margaret through the smelly gas works at Fort St. John. Almost inaudible in the din, he bored the poor thing with a half-hour discourse on pumps and rigs. He became a horseman, flying his stables by jet to the race tracks of America. He made new friends, Richard Nixon for one, his close neighbour at his "home-away-from-taxes" on Jungle Road, Palm Beach, Florida. Frank gave Dick $100,000 one time to help him become President.

Still McMahon never forgot his native province. He laid great stress on what he called "Stable Government"— nothing to do with racing. In 1960 a surging CCF was close to election victory over W.A.C. Bennett. McMahon thoughtfully assigned two of his hired persuaders to the Vancouver *Daily Province*. On the Saturday before the Monday voting, the *Province* ran black headlines:

CCF Victory Would Wreck Vast Project,
Cost 10,000 jobs

Beneath the headline McMahon allowed that the CCF
was "half-married to the Labour Bosses" and "highly
vulnerable to Communist infiltration." Without the time,
or the means, to respond, the CCF lost the election.

W.A.C. Bennett was soon allowed to express his thanks.
By that time there was enough oil in the Peace to pipe
down to Kamloops, and then to the Vancouver refineries
through existing pipelines. "Why not," said McMahon to
Bennett, "lay the oil pipeline on our existing natural gas
right of way?" Why not, indeed! And for the use of the
right of way Westcoast asked and got a mere 750,000
shares from the oil pipeline company. Those shares were
worth $15 each. A nice windfall for Westcoast for
extending the use of a right of way the government had
given it for nothing.

In 1973, the NDP was ensconced in government. It was
too late to chase the dollars that Frank McMahon and the
Pirates had made off with, although not too late to bring
future dividends to people from the people's heritage.

With joy in our hearts we broke the twenty-year contract
that gave Americans our gas for less than the cost to
British Columbians. Legislation set up the B.C. Petroleum
Corporation as a public monopoly—the sole purchaser,
and seller—of natural gas. National Energy Board
regulations were finagled; constitutional questions were
avoided with mine detectors. Incensed Americans and
fussed diplomats were stroked. The border price for gas
was promptly raised 29 cents to 58 cents per million cubic
feet.

Socred blockade in the Legislature! It was led by the
Honourable Don Phillips, now B.C.'s Minister of
Industry. There were angry denunciations of "Jack Boot
Government." Phillips, who can tell you everything he

knows in ten minutes, spoke for four hours, his Motor-Mouth on Throttle. We clocked him at 105 words per minute with gusts up to 165. "This corporation," he declaimed, "will cost the taxpayers millions and millions of dollars out of general revenue." Alas, even a financial genius can stumble. In its first operating year the Petroleum Corporation brought $92 million into general revenue; in 1981, $235 million. Since 1973 nearly a billion and a half dollars have come back to the people, who, if only for the moment, owned their own gas. We called it 30-second socialism.

Back to coal, Legs. Old King Coal is a poor old soul beside his slick and sinuous oil and gas sisters. It took coal thousands of years to depose the horse as the way to go, but only a hundred or so for coal to be dethroned by steam from oil boilers. But slowly the hour of coal was coming round again; hard coal is good for blast furnaces, soft coal for heat and electricity, all kinds of it will make, some day, pretty dresses.

B.C., the cluck, hands out coal licences the same way it issues fishing licences, first come, first served. The applicant bellies up to the counter with his map and signs an application. Mind you, a coal licence costs more than a fishing licence. You now pay $2 per acre ($5 a hectare if you're metric) for the first year's rent. In addition, to keep your licence, you have to do $3 per acre's worth of work in the first year. This work requirement (or payment in lieu thereof) rises to a maximum of $20 after ten years. These stupendous costs are the same, in constant dollars, as they were 50 years ago.

Still, the licence-holder doesn't have to worry too much about the pocket money he pays the government to keep his licences in good standing. His paper licence is negotiable—a form of legal tender—something to trade on the stock exchange or in private deals. And some B.C. coal licences have hawked very well. But were there really promoters' fortunes to be made from coal? Yes, there were, Legs. I can tell you of a man who crossed over the border with a suitcase stuffed with more green than Frank McMahon had taken south. Edgar Forsburg Kaiser is his name—coal his game. Edgar bled this province the way the old leech doctors used to bleed their patients. Leave him for a minute while I tell you about some coal licences in the Peace River coalfields.

Government geologists have long explored the coal of the Sukunka in the northeast. The public are still at work; the Legislature voted $5 million for further public surveys in 1982.

In 1970, Brameda, a private company, natch', acquired 42 coal licences in the Sukunka, around Bullmoose Mountain. Then Brameda and its licences were slowly digested by the Tech Corporation. After that came a side deal with Brascan. Finally, in January, 1977, British Petroleum paid Tech $30 million for twenty of the 42 licences. What the people gave away for a song went, part of it, for $30 million in up-front money seven years later. It was money B.P. had to find before a dollar could be spent to move coal—or to employ people. What fools we clucks be!

In the northeast, coal now comes on stream, massively subsidized by public dollars, with no public equity in the coal. In the southeast, coal has been mined for 100 years. In 1977 I rode in a Kaiser Resources jeep to the top of Balmer Mountain in the southeast, 5,500 feet above sea level. Two-hundred-ton trucks carried away the rocky overburden; hydraulic jets exposed the seams; 100-tonners trucked coal down to the washers; unit-trains, clanking their chains like ghosts in the night, 112 open cars, manned only by an engineer, a foreman and a brakeman, freighted the coal through the coast ranges to tide-water; thirteen trains a week, 100 tons in each car. The Canadian Dream fulfilled! An American company, Kaiser, mining Canadian coal, for the steel mills of Japan.

Reclamation work on top of Balmer Mountain was good. Top soil re-covered the devastated areas, trees were planted from nursery seedlings—and yet there was something fleeting, fugitive about this operation. The company headquarters at Sparwood were a string of plywood shacks, maps and statistics pinned to the walls. Kaiser would be here today and gone tomorrow—taking with it patents, research and, above all, the money to relocate elsewhere. The words of Angus MacInnis, CCF Member of Parliament for Vancouver-Kingsway, come back to me as I write. "We'd better throw an anchor into the Pacific before the multinationals tow this province out to sea." Angus resigned in 1957 and I was elected in his place. I lost the seat within nine months, before I had even located the men's washroom on Parliament Hill. Someone called John Diefenbaker began to have Visions, Northern Visions I think they were, and people took him for a seer. No one in my riding knew who John's candidate was, and party affiliation was not on the ballot. On election day voters asked me outside the polls, "Alex, what's the name of the Conservative candidate?" They would have voted for a dog; did, as a matter of fact. I was relieved of my Parliamentary duties.

The Kaiser operation began in 1967 when Kaiser Steel of Fontana, California, incorporated Kaiser Resources. CPR coal lands in the East Kootenays were purchased for $65 million. These were coal lands Canada had taken from the Indians and given to the CPR. Kaiser Resources had, of course, already negotiated its contracts for the sale of metallurgical coal to Japan. Then it borrowed $50 million from a Canadian bank as start-up money.

There were losses in the first years. Kaiser had to invent hydraulic machinery for the strip mines to prevent falling rock from pulverizing the coal. By 1973, however, Kaiser sold a 27 per cent interest—7,236,000 shares—to its Mitsubishi customers in Japan at $3.80 a share. By October, 1980, those shares were worth (at $80) $3.69

billion. It was an industrial empire, with coal worth $600 million annually crossing the Pacific Ocean to come tripping back in the form of funny little Mazdas and Toyotas.

Not something un-self-reliant Canadians could have done for themselves! Well, not considering the ways our political leaders have played it.

Kaiser Steel made Edgar Forsburg Kaiser its proconsul at Kaiser Resources. His grandfather, Henry J. Kaiser, had built Liberty Ships on the assembly line to run the blockade of Hitler's submarines. Edgar himself had become a millionaire in three generations—taking one more than Bill Bennett.

Edgar took his first stock options in Kaiser Resources by setting up a dummy company called KRC. He took these options on the sly because the first shares in Kaiser Resources could be issued only to Canadians, and Edgar was then an America. Later, he and Kaiser Steel of California gave themselves more promotional shares at cut prices. Still later, in 1972, existing shareholders of Kaiser Resources were given options to buy two and a half million shares for $2.85 each. These shares were soon worth $16 each. But the big coup was still to come.

Edgar was at home in High Society. After hearing the musical offerings of an orchestra in Switzerland, he airlifted the fifteen players to Vancouver to entertain party guests. He went into urban renewal. His four-year-old house on Belmont Drive that cost $300,000 to build was demolished. So small was the swimming pool! So old the house, that it had to be condemned! From the rubble a statelier palace rose with the help of a $925,000 interest-free loan from Kaiser Resources, which was always concerned for the welfare of its workers (Edgar was Worker No. 1). Edgar made the papers again when a judge settled a million or so on his divorced wife, and the snow tires.

The NDP government imposed a moratorium on the granting of coal licences soon after taking office, and increased coal royalties from 14 cents to $1.50 per ton. I was in Premier Dave Barrett's office when Edgar was told of the royalty increase. He took the news like a man—mumbling something about a clause in his sales contract that enabled him to pass the costs of "legislative surprises" on to his Japanese customers. Again in the fall of 1975 Edgar was called to the Premier's office. This time he was told the royalty was to be $2.50. Once more, he managed his wry smile, thinking, I am certain, "Oh, sure, $2.50 *if* you guys survive the election."

We didn't but he did, and with the election came a Christmas present from the new Premier for his tiny Edgar—cancellation of the royalty increase.

Ah, was it cancelled for good consideration? Were campaign funds given to the Social Credit, passing "privily" (pace, Shakespeare, for I'm borrowing from you)?

> *For I was sure that Edgar*
> *Paid 'ere the Socreds promised*
> *Whereby his suit was granted*
> *'Ere it was asked*

Edgar's salary and benefits were now $735,000 a year—plus dividends—and Kaiser Resources' till was flush with swelling cash reserves. Extras came in. The company bought Ashland Oil for $500 million and sold it to Dome two years later for $750 million. The coal mine was cash rich while its parent, Kaiser Steel, was crying for cash to modernize its steel mill. Something had to be done. Kaiser Resources offered to buy nine million of its own shares at $44 when the market price was only $26. Kaiser Steel tendered 4.2 million of the shares it had got for nothing for a cheque in the sum of $185 million. How touching! A corporate child rushing to the aid of its father.

And out there in 1980 was a new corporate belly full of cash, the B.C. Resources Investment Corporation. (Some of the cash came from B.C. citizens whose manners were too refined to say no to a personal invitation from the Premier.) The new corporation was created by Premier Bennett when he privatized the industrial assets acquired in the NDP years. It was known as BRIC for short, and Edgar shortly laid plans to gold-brick it.

BRIC began the mating ritual with an offer of $44 for Kaiser shares. Kaiser, which conveniently had a Director on the BRIC Board, sniffed its disdain; not enough! BRIC increased its offer to $55 for all Kaiser shares, with a sweetener added for Edgar. He was to stay on as a supersalesman to sell coal already sold. His fee: $10 million a year.

Now everyone was happy except the common people. New options were rushed out to the inner circles while the deal was brewing. The BRIC-Kaiser Director made a profit of $2.49 million on his shares. Edgar, buying more shares as the dealing progressed, cashed a cheque for $50 million. Kaiser Steel, the impecunious parent, received another $250 million, enough to complete modernization of the California steel works to ward off any Pacific coast competition, even from British Columbia.

A B.C.-Ontario Security investigation found that it simply proved that capitalism was working to full capacity.

More coal lies on the mountains, lots of it, silent, black, waiting its hour—already spoken for.

In Nelson in June, 1977, Premier Bennett announced that the ban on coal licences put on by the NDP would be lifted. There was to be, he said, "a new system of granting licences to incorporate competitive tendering." Competition? This was unheard of among the oligopolies. The Coal Association hastily called meetings with the government's Coal Committee. At the last, on February 7, 1978, the civil servants were asked to leave the room. Three days later the moratorium was lifted—but competitive bidding was out. The old system of granting licences was back—over the counter, first come, first served. First served were those who had the word.

Within three months, coal licences covering 705 square miles were taken up, all but 112 square miles by five big companies. Four of these were oil giants: Gulf with 893 licences, Esso with 87, British Petroleum with 72, Shell with 64. What a bonanza give-away of resource rights to multinational companies! Were they licences to mine? Or to keep in the deep freeze? Or to sell?

There's a postscript, Legs. The government never would have dared to give away these coal rights if the report of a Coal Task Force had been made public. No government would have had the nerve. The Coal Task Force, under the prestigious Dr. William Armstrong, head of geology at UBC, had begun its work in 1975. All MLAs had received Volume I of this Task Force report, which contained technical data. But Volume II was missing. In fact, on June 17, 1976, well before the bonanza give-away, Volume II had been delivered to the government. There, stamped "Confidential" in large black letters, thirteen copies had been distributed to selected Ministers and officials. The rest is silence—except for this: Armstrong told me that Volume II made recommendations to protect the resource against the give-away that followed. More, he told me, he could not say.

What's a poor NDP to do, Legs, when B.C. (Canada, too) has already squandered its birthright of resources?

Should we follow the Petro-Can example? That public oil company was conceived by our David Lewis and begotten of the Liberals' Pierre Trudeau. But what does paternity matter? Yes, let's have more public companies participating in industries, but not (as Petro-Can has so far) behaving like any other private company.

Should we favour incentive grants to induce private companies to explore for Arctic oil and gas? Give the well-off tax write-offs to induce them to invest? We should, not on your life. Duff would have drilled himself.

Let's face it, Legs, the cost of buying back the country is prohibitively expensive. If we can't socialize the resource rights, at least we can socialize the resource. We broke that trail with natural gas. The Apple Marketing Board gave us the idea. The grower had to sell to the Board, which in turn sold the apple.

I'd have a Coal Corporation to do the same darn thing. It wouldn't just buy and sell the coal. It would bring the industry under public control. The staff? You don't need many. Some good geologists, engineers, accountants, salespeople. It would pay producers the right price and sell to the world for the best price. We would let the Corporation deal with foreign governments or conglomerates, one on one—we sell this, and we buy that, some reciprocal trading!

If producers won't mine when they should, then their licences should be cancelled, leaving the Coal Corporation to mine, directly or under contract.

And a Timber Board, exclusive purchaser of logs from the forest—replanting trees . . . but now I wander . . . let other examples wait.

There I am, Legs, well to the right of the Sheriff of Nottingham and well to the left of the Genghis.

For "Maitre Chez Nous," Je Suis Toujours,

Yours,

Alex

ARE WE COUNTING HEADS INSTEAD OF TURNING THEM?

The Legislature
Victoria, B.C.
May 20, 1984

Dear Legs,

The Dean of the Legislature (yours truly, the longest sitting Member) is back in his seat. Members compliment him on his recovery, some as if they thought it was a fluke, he being older than he looks. Others sidle up saying, "Take it easy, Alex," and he takes advantage of this to sit in his office and write another letter. At no time does he let on that he is playing squash again, and definitely not that you beat him last Sunday (with some lucky crevice shots). Still he wonders how much longer he can get away with being an invalid.

The Legislature has resumed its leisurely pace, with Members on both sides back in their habitual, and predictable, roles. All the passion of last fall's upheavals has been spent, "for violent fires soon burn out themselves." Debate continues on the remnants of Bennett's restraint legislation, for the umpteenth time, with everyone going home at six o'clock.

I enjoy the sympathy but no longer like to be told I'm looking fine. Mark Rose spoiled that by telling me that there are Three Ages of Man: Youth, Middle Age and

"My, you're looking fine." Nor do I like "Don't you wish you were younger, Alex?" I have Conrad Adenhauer's words ready for the next time I get that one. At 85, still Chancellor of Germany, and down with the grippe, he replied testily, "No, I don't want to be younger, I just want to keep on getting older."

I have thanked the Members who sent me get-well messages in the hospital, including one Socred, the ghoul, who sent a card wishing me "God Speed." And I couldn't resist tweeking my colleagues by telling them about an NDPer they know who paid me a bedside visit. He is itching to run in my seat and said, "Oh, Alex, you're coming along fine, you'll run again, and again." I thanked him and asked if he'd mind taking his thumb off my drainage tube. Good stories, Legs, like to be retreaded and to stretch.

Ed Broadbent came to our Caucus yesterday to inform us that Utopia would be a little late this spring. The NDP has just been given 13 per cent in the national Gallup Poll, a record low. Our Ed, however, showed his mettle, assuring us that the bounding little decimal had nowhere to go but up. I think so too. With any luck our poor Ed will be up against two rich glamour boys in the election, Bay Street and St. James Street, with a difference between them you could put in your eye, Tweedle-urner and Tweedle-oney. I just hope those striped pants run neck and neck.

Ed's visit prompts me to write about how the NDP should campaign, during and between elections. First I'll talk about our basic principles and how much of them we should lay on the line; second, about electioneering methods; and third, about the programs with which we fight particular elections, and how they must be convincing and different if the NDP is to justify its presence on the political scene. I may even toss in some political advice to an aspiring young politician (you), which I have figured out too late for it to be of any use to me.

So settle in for a footloose, rambling letter, Legs, with one broad message. The message is that the NDP can't go on just responding with short-term, knee-jerk quick fixes to whatever comes up, responses, by the way, that are often emotional and almost always opportunistic. We spout cliches because we are not thinking things through. Don't tell me we have to and that people won't listen to anything but platitudes in the age of the 30-second TV clip. I don't believe it. Our arguments can cut deeper and we can present the hard solutions and long-term directions many Canadians are looking for. Later I'll illustrate my point with two examples: one, science, by far the most important force shaping our lives; the other, world peace, without which we won't have any lives to shape. So that's what's coming, and if you finish this letter before I do, be my guest!

Ed's talk about our popularity rating brought back nostalgic memories of spring, 1943, when the CCF had a Gallup of 29 per cent, yes, 29 per cent, and it achieved this in spite of (or because of) being strikingly different from the Old Parties, and letting its principles hang out for anyone to inspect before buying. Even by 1940 the CCF was so strong in B.C. that the Liberals and Conservatives were forced to crawl under the same blanket for mutual protection. There they carried on their internecine warfare by other means. Such memories give me a twinge in my long tooth. For since those days the CCF-NDP has been cruelly becalmed. Like the Ancient Mariner, we sure could use a breeze to breathe, or preferably a roaring wind to take us to where we should be by this time anyway.

Socialist movements everywhere are in a quandary, one that faced the CCF in 1943 and faces the NDP today. It is, how much in the way of principles should be spent, or thrown away, in order to win votes? Some NDPers panic and want to jettison most of our ballast to try to get moving again.

J.S. Woodsworth, the father of the CCF (and so the grandfather of the NDP), wouldn't spend any of his principles to win elections. By 1943, however, he no longer sat at the head of the table when the CCF Caucus met, no longer the stern Jehovah whose word was law. The CCF had a new leader in M.J. Coldwell and began to pay more attention to the crude realities of practical politics.

I met J.S. Woodsworth in Winnipeg in 1938 when I was a delegate to a Conference of the Student Christian Movement. I wasn't much of a student Christian but had already, although a Son of a Bencher, been bitten by the socialist bacillus (in the head, not in the stomach, for I did nothing about it). Woodsworth's presence at the conference still burns brightly in my memory. He had travelled, as usual, from Ottawa by day coach, munching sandwiches his wife had made, with no visits to the dining car, and sleeping bolt upright in his hard seat.

In a dingy classroom he denounced the sale of Canadian scrap iron to feed the blast furnaces of the Japanese War Lords, who were marching into China. Courtly and polite, he spoke with the savage indignation of an Old Testament prophet, white goatee bobbing as he emphasized his points, though he never flailed his arms or pointed a finger. He played a role (himself) without any mask. The sales meant jobs in Canada but that didn't count for him when they contributed to the spilling of blood.

Woodsworth had none of the political guile of his opponent, Mackenzie King, the Liberal Leader. King didn't care where he was going as long as he was in the driver's seat. With Woodsworth, destination was everything. His opponents understood him. In 1935 the Liberal Government had moved in the Commons to strip away the voting rights of the Doukhobors who had settled in the Kootenays—not because their women sometimes stripped in the courts or because their radical sect sometimes burned houses; it was simply because they refused to be enumerated in the Census. In the debate, Woodsworth spoke eloquently for equal citizenship rights. Across the Chamber, Ian Mackenzie, Liberal Member for Vancouver Centre, listened intently. Finally he pounced with a quiet interjection. "Is the Honourable Member in favour of enfranchising the Orientals in British Columbia?" Woodsworth replied with a simple "yes." The Liberals, like jubilant delinquents, took out full-page ads in the Vancouver papers setting out that little exchange from Hansard. Their pandering to prejudice won them votes and cost the CCF seats in the election that followed.

Woodsworth, by the way, was just as scrupulous about raising money as winning votes. Once, after a meeting at Massey Hall in Toronto, he was presented with a cheque to the CCF for $5,000 by a man who had been deeply moved by his speech. He promptly handed it back. No one should have such a sizable interest in the socialist movement! Today? Quick, the receipt book!

The CCF was unquestionably Canada's conscience under Woodsworth. He was gone by the time I joined. On a brisk March day in 1942 his ashes had been scattered from a small boat on the sun-flecked waters of Georgia Strait. At a memorial service his faithful disciple, Bill Irvine, spoke of his "supersensitivity to another's pain" and of what set him apart from the run of politicians. "Woodsworth *was*," he told the hushed throng, "what he seemed to be and he was *that* all the way through, everywhere and always."

Irvine fought on, losing more elections than he won. He wrote a play in which a character called McGregor (obviously J.S.) was given the lines:

> It is true that we cannot win socialism without first winning the election. But it is just as true that we

might win the election in such a way as to lose
socialism . . . I cannot permit any modification of
policy with a view to getting votes.

This was, I am afraid, Legs, a counsel of both perfection
and defeat. There are two strains in the CCF-NDP
movement, one idealistic, the other pragmatic, and we
need some of each. Woodsworth represented the first with
his belief that truth and righteousness are bound to
triumph in time if we stick by them. The other strain, with
which we are all too familiar, takes us down into the barrel
with the other polecats to give truth and righteousness a
helping hand. This we do by adopting Parliamentary
tactics whose object is to embarrass our opponents; by
following public opinion instead of leading it; by flogging
popular issues to the exclusion of some that really matter;
and by appealing to interest groups over the heads of just
plain citizens.

There is a needle, in political parties as in individuals,
that tries to steal across the dial from youthful idealism to
winning as an end in itself. We have to keep an eye on it,
and, yes, be prepared to spend some principle from time to
time, but not to pay such a high price to win power that we
lose our reason for existence.

I'll tell you how we can be realistic without giving up our
goals, although it seems pretty obvious. At elections our
job is to try to persuade people to come with us at least as
far as the next station, while making it clear that this
station is just one way-stop on a route that leads to our
destination. Nor should we be mealy-mouthed about that
destination, even during elections. We should say that we
stand, finally, for a clean break with a system in which
private profit expectations determine what people make or
do, and which shape their relations with each other; and
that we stand for a system where all will be relatively free
and equal because each has a stake in the country.

And before I break out of my highfalutin mood, let me say that what Woodsworth left behind was his insistence that we can't have or win a new social order without a change in people's attitudes. There are Marxists around who hold that some historical clash of classes will inexorably produce a free and just society. The truth is that reforming society and enlarging people's concern for one another have to go forward together.

All right, I'll come along quietly, down from the pulpit and tell you how the NDP should campaign, and why it should stop trying to copy our opponents' election gimmicks and psephological techniques. (How's that? Easy! From "psephos," the pebble the Athenians dropped in an urn to vote.) I admit it's scary to think about the evolving election techniques the NDP is already up against. Even now our cash-heavy opponents go into elections carefully programmed by media consultants. They use motivational experts and sophisticated polling. And their advertising contains hidden persuaders that cleverly play on the hopes and fears of the electorate. Already they merchandise their candidates as if they were deodorants and treat the voters as if they were marching ants or Pavlov's salivating dogs. The U.S. Republican Party has the latest gimmick, an automatic telephone that dials at random and "talks" to the poor voter and hangs up on him if it finds he is committed to Walter Mondale! Still, I think socialists should keep their faith in individuality and refuse to play these 1984 election games; better we should blow the whistle on them and expose them for what they are. If Bill Bennett coughs up whatever this modest opus will cost, he'll be glad to read these words. But his cynical manipulations will carry him only as far as the next election. Our principles will take us further.

In the first place, those election tricks are too expensive for us and we will never be able to match what the Big Business Establishment will spend in defence of its privileges. In the second place, our hearts won't be in those election games because deep down we despise them.

How then, you well may ask, can the NDP hope to defend itself, let alone win? Only by becoming even more of a people's movement than it is now, with lots of guerrilla partisans in the constituencies, motivated by conviction, conversing, knocking on doors, spelling out particular hopes and dangers. And how do we get more partisans, Legs? By having principles that appeal to something beyond selfish advantage and policies that are not mindless and trivial.

Let me tell you tales of a few campaigns, two in 1960 brimming with vitality, and one last year methodical and inert. The first was my election to the Legislature from Vancouver East in 1960. That was a campaign of Joy and Substance, with the CCF standing for more than it was against, and setting out what it stood for with a decent respect for the intelligence of the voters. I enjoyed that campaign. We had to win back one of the two East seats that had been lost to the Socreds in 1956. Our workers were just a happy few compared with the numbers of today and we had barely enough money to pay the printer. Yet we set out on a spirited crusade. "Cheerly to sea, the signs of war advance!" We took to the streets, a theatrical troupe of children, dogs, old-timers and girls in bright sashes, stopping to talk to any voter who was seen sitting on his stoop or working his garden. Our literature demanded the socialization of the B.C. Electric Company and proudly and in detail proclaimed its sins and the benefits of public power, complete with graphs and cartoons. We couldn't canvass many homes or "pull" the vote on election day but everyone knew we had been around, alive and kicking, and they turned out to vote because we had lit a fire in their bellies. We almost knocked over W.A.C. Bennett and did make him take over the B.C. Electric before he went to the people again.

Not far away in 1960, Dave Barrett, running for the first time, drew a potent weapon from his arsenal, infectious drollery. Dave was Jewish (still is I think) and had the redoubtable task of cracking the French-Catholic vote in Maillardville. He did it by inveigling the town's Good Catholic Father into saying that "while Barrett was not a Catholic, at least he wasn't a Protestant." The Word was spread through the Flock. Joy wins more hearts and minds than sullen sincerity or anger. Good speakers know that their message is getting across when both they and their audience are having a good time.

Last May's election in Vancouver East was a grimmer affair and I was glad when it was over. It was the cautious, methodical campaign we are getting used to in the NDP, unfortunately. All the candidates were supposed to be saying the same thing, and at that as little as possible. (When you are that cautious and someone does make a blooper it goes off like a bomb!) We had more workers and money than in 1960, enough money, in fact, to pay a campaign manager and four or five sub-managers, causing resentment among other volunteers who often worked just as hard. Committee rooms were crammed with people with sore eyes, transcribing names and addresses into walking order for the canvassers to call on. The canvassers slogged from door to door and turned in sheets with "markings" showing who was for us, who against, and marking as "doubtful" the guy who was furious at being taken from his TV set. Neither Markers nor Markees were really comfortable in the process. The Markers left behind a slick, four-colour, bonded Central Leaflet. It was easy on the eyes, with pictures of the Leader and the Candidate baring their teeth, and easy on the brain too for there was nothing in it to manure anyone's mind. In 200 words it explained that the NDP was in favour of health, jobs and education, as if someone, somewhere out there, wasn't. Of course, some Socreds really weren't, but their leaflet was no different from ours, including the teeth.

Our issues had been selected by polls that cost NDP Headquarters $60,000 each, and came in two months after the pulses had been felt. The polls, expensive elaborations of the obvious, revealed well-known secrets that anyone could find out over the back fence. Try asking a man who you wouldn't pay to do a day's work what the big issue is and he'll say "unemployment."

I had argued for an eight-page special election edition of the NDP provincial newspaper, the *Democrat*. Such a paper can challenge the voters with meaningful stories about the issues, in short punchy paragraphs, with headlines for those who won't read more, and cartoons and graphics and fun; brain food that would include an appreciation of the problems of leaner, harder years as well as their possibilities; and an appeal to pull together and give something up, if need be, in the general public interest. My argument kept getting lost somewhere in the Election Planning Committee.

Oh, the vote was good on election day and we pulled out some around the province who wouldn't have bothered to vote. So did the Socreds. Ironically, we were killed by a high turnout, toppled by quite a few who feared the unknown, not quite believing in our new, safe image. In the last days, little though we knew it, our "markings" were slipping invisibly across the sheets from "for" to "doubtful" to "against."

The NDP originated systematic door-to-door canvassing in the late 1960s, three knocks on each door, primary, secondary and tertiary treatment of the voter. Today all parties, with grim intensity, try to get a fix on everyone's intentions. Phone banks increasingly replace the door-to-door canvass. Happily there are fractious individuals who refuse to let on what they are really thinking. There are even some rotten souls who are born deceivers. If their numbers improve, politics may be driven back into neighbourhood coffee parties where the state of things can be intelligently assessed. That's a consummation the NDP should encourage. Instead too many NDPers want the Party to invest in computers and softwear to feed everyone's likes and dislikes into. Not mine they won't! I'll lie first. We're already too hung up on identifying votes instead of winning them.

I prefer the flying canvass, preferably with the candidate in a small group, hitting the voter when he's visible, in a natural encounter, in a shopping centre or on his porch. Never, Legs, ask him right out how he will vote, for that's his business, and he will let you know if he wants to. Many you'll never get a fix on.

I failed to get a fix on one man sitting on his back porch in his undershirt in 1963. As I bounded up his stairs, he disappeared into the kitchen. I skidded around on his freshly painted porch until he reappeared with a "Wet Paint" sign and spattered me with choice profanities. Hiding my copy of the CCF *News* I beat a fast retreat, calling back, "Don't forget your Social Credit candidate on election day."

Whatever did politicians do before polling? One, W.A.C. Bennett, the complete politician, had a better feel for what people thought than any polling could give him. In the elevator, or the barber shop, with bellboys or taxi drivers, he brought up politics—and listened. He also had gumshoes moseying around and reporting back. His office was littered with papers, city and country, because he read every letter to every editor.

W.A.C. knew how to make political hay out of little occasions. Once he went into the Kaslo Hotel beer parlour where the hard hats who were building the High Arrow Dam refreshed themselves. He told his side-kick, Wes Black, to order drinks all round, with Wes' $20 bill, yet, for as a total abstainer W.A.C. wouldn't buy alcohol! He was as tight as his son. A week later Wes was told that each hard hat had kept his glass "that the Premier bought for me."

All encounters, by the way, are not as fortuitous. Jim Fulton, our brown bear of an MP from Skeena, had to fight his way up the path past the snarling black dog to talk politics with the old couple in their home. The dog followed him in. Talking earnestly, Jim was astonished to see the dog lift its leg and leave a yellow pool on the carpet. Still the old couple continued to listen to their MP as if nothing had happened. Except that, as Jim was leaving, the husband inquired plaintively, "Are you not taking your dog with you?" A partly true story, Legs.

NDPers should help people develop a resistance to pollsters. After all, even the mosquito acquired an immunity to DDT. The rich use polls to pick the minds of the poor, when they're not picking their pockets. Poll questions can be devious, such as a recent one that asked, "In these times do you favour cutting back on Old Age Pensions or on Social Welfare?" That pollster, anonymous as usual, wanted to read the voter's head rather than get a square answer to an honest question. Sure, we can school people, Legs, to become consummate liars, many layered ones, when confronted with questions like that. But why not pick up what people are thinking in the old-fashioned way, by talking to them! The Socreds' Big Blue Machine would say that that approach is too time-consuming, and the responses usually jam up the computer.

The more we lack confidence in the programs we put forward, the more we revert to counting heads instead of turning them. The NDP promises, as it has to do, much the same things as the other parties—jobs, health, peace and so on—with many thinking we can't deliver those things any better than the other parties. A few nights ago I watched an NDP speaker come on with an empty promise on national free-time TV. He put the NDP firmly on record against high interest rates. Those rates, however, are a symptom of other things that are wrong in the economy, and while he attacked the symptom he did not attack the causes, let alone propound a cure. High interest rates are one way (the falling dollar is another) by which a country pays for its mistakes—living beyond its means; not investing enough in the productive sector; not controlling costs; and inefficiencies in competitive export industries. Some belts, quite a few of them, have to be tightened to get at those causes, and our spokesman wasn't about to suggest that. Nor did he suggest that the cost of money will bob up and down until the economy is subjected to some pretty rigorous public planning. I think our audiences, Legs, have more common sense than we give them credit for. We're too anxious to please everyone and stroke every politically significant interest group. Hear this! The party that has no enemies loses its friends. Even God had to invent the Devil in order to give Himself credibility.

Some day you'll be a better candidate than that speaker of ours, Legs. So learn and listen! If the face in the bathroom mirror smiles at you, smile back at it. Then, by all means, hit the streets with a "high opinion of yourself." (That's what Bob Hawke, Labour Prime Minister of Australia, says he has of himself.) If you remember your name, use it. When in doubt tell the truth. If you keep telling people what they want to hear they'll think you have false teeth. When you foul up admit it. The only good time to give out bad news is yesterday. Level with people so you don't become like Lloyd George who, in his later years, was said to inspire every emotion except trust. And don't bore people by compressing the most words into the fewest ideas. This is an instant age. Remember that it takes longer to prepare a short speech than a long one. When you do speak, burn some fuel and don't let your decibel count creep up to the falsetto; use your diaphragm.

You can carry a notebook of names and faces but don't let anyone see it. I have never kept one, but Paul Martin, former Liberal Minister of Everything, did and would have wiped me if I had run against him when I lived in Windsor. Paul did not suffer a sparrow to fall in his constituency without his special notice. Births, graduations, weddings and deaths received his courteous congratulations. Only once, so the story goes, did he trip up. After greeting a voter with, "Ah, Mr. Podovinckoff, and how is your lovely wife, Mabel?", he got the reply, "Oh, she's still dead."

Too much of this! I'd better get to electioneering or next I'll tell you how to exercise your mouth so you'll have an elastic one like Rene Levesque's. I have made winning seem easier for the NDP than it really is. When you run you'll know soon enough that NDP elections are fought in an unfriendly context. That context is the prevailing ethics which affect most aspects of North American society— acquisitiveness, insensitivity and looking out for No. 1. That makes it hard for us to promote our counter values of mutuality and the fair sharing of benefits and burdens for the good of all. All we can do is to express those values, clearly and confidently, wherever and whenever we can.

And let's not kid ourselves that we can turn values around by finding the money to buy better shelf space for our election wares or fancier packaging for our programs. The NDP should stop wasting money on billboards (with a logo!) and five-voice singing commercials, because these things say nothing except that we are a party just like the others. The thinner our ideas the more we fall back on sales techniques. It reminds me of you, Legs, thinking you can beat me if only you had a better squash racquet. Well, you can't afford a better one, and besides, the game's the thing! So let the other parties go with their media consultants and image manipulators while we of the emerging counter-culture expose them by letting people know what they are up to. In the words of the Anthem, "Confound their Politics, Frustrate their Knavish Tricks, even, if all else fails, poke fun at them!"

As I said, elections are determined on two planes. On one level the public judges the parties on the issues and the promises they put forward; on the other level the public judges those who stand behind the issues and promises, their character, values, integrity, ability to respond in an emergency. On this level the object is to win trust and respect and that comes, finally, by being what you really are and saying what you really mean.

Socialist values and ideas have a better chance of catching on where the humanities, history, literature and the arts are widely taught and enjoyed. So it is not surprising that socialists instinctively advance and defend the cause of liberal education. What is surprising is that the self-same socialists are just as instinctively apt to fear and distrust the serious contributions of science and new technology.

Their benighted right-wing adversaries, quite the other way, are apt to be more receptive to new technology while instinctively suspicious of education in the wide-ranging humanities. Their instincts reflect their interests. A teacher with the flair to stir up minds, especially those in young skulls, to question, sift and ponder, is bound to be subversive of old ways and standing privileges. It's not surprising, therefore, that Bill Bennett's restraint axe cuts more deeply into the courses that teach the humanities than those that turn out what he calls "income producing graduates."

I've had my fill, Legs, of Socred speeches decrying what is said to be a "decline in the quality of education" and talking about the need to "restore discipline in the schools." Perhaps the Socreds' attitude toward education can be explained by the fact that they fled it at an early age. Crusty Tories have always said that their young generations were going to the dogs. I don't believe it about the young people I run into. Not long ago I spoke to a noon meeting of students at Gladstone High School. They were, with few exceptions, polite, curious, intent and very concerned about the kind of world into which they would graduate. And, bear in mind that Gladstone, like other high schools, has a higher retention rate (fewer drop-outs) than at any time in the past.

Yes, privilege ought to be chary of a teacher with the zip to get young minds into a work such as Plato's *Republic*; or into reading the *Utopia* of the Catholic martyr Sir Thomas More. "For who knoweth not," wrote Sir Thomas, "that fraud, theft, raping, brawling, chiding, murder . . . do die when money dieth." Wise old owls like Sir Thomas turn young heads. Stand-patters, beware! Ah, do they secretly yearn, some of those blinkered reactionaries, for the good old days of yore, with Gentlemen and Peasants, when to the unlettered Ploughboy:

> *Knowledge to his eyes*
> *Her ample Scroll*
> *Rich with the Spoils of Time,*
> *Did ne'er unroll*

The B.C. Minister of Education declines to define the purposes of education. Surely the primary purpose is the enrichment of lives. The second is the cultivation of the civilities that make good citizenship. The third is instruction in those skills that enable human beings to wrest comfortable lives from nature.

Still, why should we blame the Minister? How many of us pause to reflect upon the purposes of society itself? All too readily we fall into the assumption that industrialized societies exist for the acquisition of material wealth, period. Economic goals are important, but remain only one element among those that make human existence unique and worth living. Remember Socrates: "The unexamined life is not worth living." It makes you ponder where the Socred horse is pulling the cart of education.

But why, Legs, are our fellow socialists so skittish about science? Too often they, and we, approach such questions as the fluoridation of the water supply, waste disposal, the tiny atom or big plans for a dam in the mountains with more of the heat of passion than the light of insight. We're downright conservative, we fellows are, as if our conversion to socialism had used up our capacity for innovation. Was it ever so? I stumbled on a little speech of a Mr. Creevy, a famous radical of his day, in which in 1825 he expressed his relief to a Committee of the British Parliament. "The Devils of Railways," he said, "have been strangled at last. That infernal nuisance, the Loco-Monster, carrying eight tons of goods and navigated by a tail of smoke and sulphur, coming through everyman's grounds."

Modern science shouldn't scare us. It's the use to which the results of scientific discovery are being put that should scare the daylights out of us and that's because politics is failing to control and direct those uses. Socialists above all should feel at home with the methods of science, the free spirit of scientific inquiry, and should be the first to insist upon the application of that method to the solution of social problems.

I think there was more of what David Suzuki calls "an enormous respect for science" among young radicals when I was growing up. I, for one, took for granted that only science and socialism working in harness could banish poverty and disease and clean up the environment. In those days, 40 years ago, there were dirty pea souper fogs in Vancouver, so dense that I remember walking home holding onto the fender of a slow moving car. The fogs have gone as technical advances replaced sawdust burners in homes and factories with oil and gas and electricity. What, did I hear you say that today we smell better chemicals? Fair enough, but only better politics, directing the discovery and use of better techniques, can clean up the pollutants of industrialization, freshen the air and de-pollute the Fraser River.

Way back then our discussion groups had both scientific and social questions on the agendas. At one, in Vancouver after the war, a French Catholic Father himself resorted to oracular scientific proofs to defend his position. He was stoutly upholding the doctrine of the bodily Assumption of Mary into the Heavens and silenced his sceptics by finally remarking, "Well, zay never found zee bodee."

The most awesome advance of applied science occurred in 1945 when atomic fission raised the lethal mushroom cloud over Hiroshima. No other invention has been so fraught with peril, and, dare I say it, promise for mankind. Henry A. Wallace, the left-leaning Vice President of the United States, actually hailed the advent of what he said could be "Atoms for Peace." In the explosive might of unseen particles of matter he saw energy in abundance to free impoverished lives from drudgery and to de-salinate the seas in order to irrigate crops for starving millions. A woman combing the parched earth south of the Sahara for sticks and dung to make a fire, or trudging daily miles to fetch a jar of fetid water for her children, would surely agree.

I sat sulking at an NDP convention a few years ago while an emotionally charged panel of very incensed citizens flogged the Old Devil Atom for more than an hour. I sulked because no one could put that genie back in the bottle no matter how hard they tried and we should have been discussing safeguards and peaceful uses. I fell into another fret in the Legislature in 1980 when NDPers and Socreds joined in an orgy of smug self-satisfaction to impose a seven-year moratorium on uranium exploration.

Those votes repudiated the findings of Dr. Bates, a distinguished scientist. Why did the Legislature vote as it did? One-book environmentalists had whipped up popular fears of radiation and the politicians rushed to fall in line with the people . . . because they were their leaders. Those environmentalists are romantics who put the preservation of eco-systems too far ahead of the interest of the only creature that can look before and after.

Don't mistake me, Legs. I am not putting my housekeeping seal of approval on this or that nuclear generating station; simply asking that technical matters be assessed with a decent respect for knowledge, specialized as it has to be. And, no, I am not suggesting that laymen accept everything the experts say, for they often disagree among themselves, and sometimes have an axe to grind. I suggest only that laymen and women, and politicians particularly, pay attention to the consensus of the best scientific opinions before making decisions. And there are, you know, organizations of scientists committed to socially responsible applications of scientific knowledge. The politicians' consensus is usually to ignore these groups.

Clearly the space satellite Earth is a dangerous place to spend one's life or take a job. As old dangers disappear— the steam boiler that used to blow up workers is now so safe it doesn't have to be watched—new ones take their place. The woods of British Columbia still yield an annual quota of loggers killed and maimed. There are large corporations that have knowingly allowed the lungs of employees to be invaded by invisible carcinogenic asbestos fibres. Oxides of sulphur and nitrogen from smoke stacks in Sudbury kill maples in Quebec. Lurking dangers include radioactive wastes and their half-lives, a problem still waiting a safe solution. And, above all else, computer error or a faulty chip can trigger a nuclear war to end all wars, forcing everyone under the bargaining table. Way under. On the good side of the scientific ledger, mothers

no longer tell children not to go swimming for fear of
polio, automatic washers and the rest free women from
much drudgery our grandmothers faced, and the average
life span in British Columbia (not, alas, for Native
Indians) is 74 years and climbing. We humans are fated to
pursue knowledge. Even on his deathbed Goethe called for
"Light, more Light." Life remains a daunting, dizzying
adventure. Really, who wants horses to kitten or dogs to
foal? Yet, can we therefore cut off genetic research? No. A
laboratory closed in one country will open in another.

One problem is that scientists live in a separate world
from other folk. Starting in schools and universities,
budding scientists are split off from the humanities while
other students are not given an understanding of the
sciences. You find the same dichotomy in Parliaments
where Members make important decisions with no
appreciation of their scientific implications. Two soli-
tudes! I'd like to see more scientists come out of their
specialized labs, pick up a history book and get into the
political bear-pits. There they'll not have the polite
reception they are used to in academic circles, but,
dammit, there they're needed.

The bigger problem, however, is that scientific research
is not enrolled in the service of people. Some half of the
scientists today, many of them in universities, are working
for some war machine or other. Most of the others are
serving the profit dictates of private corporations. Too few
are employed in public labs where the only purpose is the
health and prosperity of human beings. I'll come to the
war machines later. Now I suggest that the old socialist
slogan about production for need instead of profit is as
valid as it ever was. The results of scientific experimenta-
tion will not be as good and safe as they should be until the
scientists involved are primarily engaged in furthering the
general welfare, not now among their top priorities.

I'd like to see NDPers take a more scientific approach to

the resolution of conflicts between growth and the environment. We have a reputation for digging up any number of reasons why developments, especially large ones, should be put on hold for further study. Not that we are as bad as some of the Greens who oppose any growth. Still, we do come on as advocates for the environment rather than as judges with a responsibility to decide where the interests of the whole community lie.

Applying the scientific method to these questions simply means doing our sums properly. Projects have both environmental advantages and disadvantages, and it's surprising how many of the disadvantages can be turned around if some extra money is spent. Balance sheets should be drawn up, with debits and credits, each carefully weighed, and the whole totalled up to reflect the interests of the many far-away as well as the interests of the nearby, and, yes, also the interests of those still to be born. Cant phrases, such as "Small is Beautiful," belong in the waste paper basket. (Get a big one!) Small though can indeed be beautiful, as in labour intensive job creation enterprises, but small can also price industries out of the competitive market place and often doesn't fit in a world of five billion.

In the 1960s the B.C. NDP paid a big political price for its reflex aversion to large developments and its tendency to pay too much attention to aggressive minority interests. I'll never forget, if I live to be normal, the day and night Sessions of the Legislature when the NDP Members manfully opposed W.A.C. Bennett's massive Two River hydro projects, the Peace and the Columbia. Some of the survivors of those debates still deplore both developments, as they do the Fall of Babylon. There were, naturally, points either way, flooding of arable land on the Arrow Lakes, for example, set beside, as it should have been, flood prevention in Trail. All the while W.A.C. Bennett had the common sense of the people with him, and he thumped the NDP soundly with his Two Rivers in three provincial elections. "Nothing is freer than free," he used to thunder, claiming that the money from the Americans in payment for downstream benefits would finance the construction costs of the dams. He was wrong, and yet those kilowatts from the Columbia are needed now in homes and industries, and are cheap compared to the costs of generating them today.

Canadian drawing boards may have no more mega-hydro projects, as capacities exceed demands and nuclear technology improves. Still, whatever megas are proposed, let's not shy away from them with simplistic slogans. In the Hungry Thirties Franklin Roosevelt built the huge Tennessee Valley dams to generate electricity, breed fishes, irrigate fields, stem floods, lay out parks and recreational areas and put a chicken in the pots of construction workers. I know it's all too easy to go for jobs *now* regardless of eco-consequences and all too hard to persuade consumers to forego plastic gadgets and electric pencil sharpeners. Nevertheless, until the NDP sums up all of the credits and debits, with the public looking on, it will deserve its present reputation of being hard on industry and soft on ecology.

Simple slogans are not answers. Peace, to take an important example, is good for ecology but bad for business. Winning a secure peace is anything but easy. Why, Legs, does not fervent NDP support for world peace translate, to the extent it should, into votes at election time? Peace policies, too, must have bottom.

There are two stages on the road to the peaceful world we want. For the first we must have policies to meet the immediate threat of thermonuclear war in the rogue world as it presently exists. For the second, long-term stage, having bought precious time, we must have policies that waste none of it in promoting a world order in which the root causes of war will be eliminated.

I am afraid, Legs, dealing with the immediate threat, that while few doubt our sincerity many doubt our practicality. Many feel that the NDP pushes into the background the dangerous realities of present international politics and fails to test its policies by the one question that urgently matters above all others. That question is whether this or that step makes World War III more or less likely. It goes without saying that a major nuclear conflict will obliterate civilized life, with only the unlucky surviving. Nothing therefore compels everyone to think more calmly. Moral revulsion against weapons and war cannot be allowed to cloud judgment. The primrose path to a nuclear holocaust may be paved with the best of intentions. Read on.

Would banning the testing of Cruise missiles in Canada make World War III more or less likely? Would unilateral nuclear disarmament by the western powers put off that war or bring it closer? Would Canada's leaving NATO, a decision somewhere among NDP convention resolutions, heighten or lessen the prospects for world peace? Would a freeze on any new nuclear arms, accepted by east and west, with verifiable controls, make war less likely? I'll stand these questions down till later.

The lucky thing going for us is that wars seldom start unless one side or the other thinks it can win. But nuclear deterrence is the chief, perhaps only, factor preventing the outbreak of World War III. A short 21 years elapsed from the end of World War I to the beginning of World War II. Thirty-nine years have now gone by since the end of World War II. That period has seen the Cold War, the Korean conflict, the Berlin Blockade, the Cuban missile crisis, the repression of Hungary, the invasion of Afghanistan and more, with the super-powers nevertheless respecting each other's vital interests; and the nuclear card continues to be considered unplayable.

It will continue to be considered unplayable only if the truths and consequences of today are constantly proclaimed. We've survived the nuclear past, which is 40 years old. Can we survive the nuclear future, which is eternal? The stark realities are simple enough even for generals, and certainly for ordinary folk, to grasp. The nuclear arsenals of east and west do not afford protection but ensure only that their adversaries, too, will not survive a major conflict. Notions of nuclear superiority are meaningless because the losses on either side will be too much to bear if only a single missile gets through, and more than a single missile will. And a conventional war (unbearable in itself, given up to date firepower) will become a nuclear war as one side loses ground. Even if all nuclear weapons were destroyed under an International Treaty, and their infernal secrets buried deeply in the earth, man's evil genius would re-create the weapons before a conventional war had run its course.

So here we are, Legs, in this year of grace, 1984, enjoying a precarious respite from World War III. I can almost see across the strait from Victoria the base at Bangor, Washington, home of the latest Trident II submarines. Each is equipped with up to 24 state-of-the-arts missiles; each missile has up to fifteen multiple war-heads; each release is programmed for accurate target delivery; the whole, in sum, giving each of the submarines 2,800 times the destructive power of the single atomic bomb that fell on Hiroshima. These frightening new weapons do not mean that east and west are getting ready to attack one another but they leave us all nonetheless in a most ticklish situation. There are some in the capitals of the major powers who fantasize about "prevailing" in nuclear war. Hollywood producers turn a dollar with films rancid with xenophobia. The outrageous costs of the war machines inflict unendurable privations erupting in regional brushfire wars. And missile response time has become so short that a master computer in Moscow or Washington may decide man's fate.

Banning Cruise missile testing in Canada would be a satisfying symbolic gesture of protest without altering the general outlook appreciably. (It would be more than symbolic, however, if enough other nations followed suit to influence the super-powers.) Taking Canada out of NATO makes no sense, for it's better to be at the table and join in the talk, when one's bacon will be fried anyway if anyone's is; and besides, NATO and the Warsaw Pact are stabilizing factors and talk back and forth in their own peculiar lexicon. Unilateral nuclear disarmament can upset the delicate balance of nuclear deterrence and cause the very evil it was designed to prevent. A freeze, however, on the development and deployment of nuclear weapons would give breathing space in which to negotiate reductions in the nuclear stockpiles and lower the levels of fear and distrust. Reversing the nuclear arms race, alas, will be as . . . well, it's really impossible to find an accurate simile since nothing is as dangerous. (Samuel Goldwyn said of the bomb in the 40s, "That thing's dynamite.") The freeze represents a practical first step, with wide support, including approval by the Committees of Catholic Bishops in Canada and the United States.

With luck human beings have time, only time, in their race with catastrophe. The other stage, building enduring peace, cannot be put off. The underlying causes of war multiply in poverties and disparities, with all of the fears, hatreds and insecurities they engender. Each passing year is a bloodstained almanac of so-called little wars and civil insurrections. The democratic socialist principles of commonwealth are badly needed within the whole human family. That's a tall order, and I'll not be around to see the day, and you, Legs, may have to content yourself with just reporting progress. Fortunately, the NDP, in sketching the broad brushstrokes of a peaceful international order, to be propagated and offered to Canadians, will not be alone. For the NDP is one of 62 parties making up the Socialist

International, each recognizing that peace is more than the absence of war; each beleaguered, as the NDP is, and yet unbowed.

There was a long ago hopeful time when I was a presence, of no importance whatsoever, at the epicentre of world affairs. In the spring of 1945, as World War II was drawing to a close, the hopes and fears of the war-torn millions met in San Francisco to found the United Nations. I remember thinking as the conference progressed that mankind stood on the threshold of a new world order. So I am excused, I take it, for continuing to dream the not impossible dream of a world with rules, rudimentary as they might be, which nation states must observe, with the penalty of sanctions if they do not, and with elementary planning of the international economy to bring health, food and education to every citizen of the globe.

I pause, to catch my breath, and to tell you how I got to San Francisco, and how Dief, later the Chief, did too, because I can't resist adding that. Prime Minister Mackenzie King, in a showy display of non-partisanship, had made my boss, CCF Leader Coldwell, a member of the Canadian delegation. I got to go with him as a gofer because my umbilical ties to the Liberal Establishment had not been wholly severed. My Aunt Nellie whispered my name in King's ear, and I went.

Diefenbaker was then the Member of Parliament for Lake Centre, poor on $4,000 a year. Already, however, he possessed the royal jelly, which in sports is called "desire," that was to propel him to the top of the greasy pole of politics. He arrived by train during the conference, red-eyed from sleeping up, eager to be able to say that he had been one among that gathering of distinguished world statesmen. King's delegation flatly refused to give this political upstart a ticket to one of the plenary sessions in the Opera House, so our future Prime Minister came to me, like a forlorn hound dog, entreating my seat. I took off for a burlesque show and Dief later rumbled to rapt audiences how he had sat behind Jan Smuts, and watched that eminent person scrawl the opening words of the Declaration of Human Rights on the back of an envelope.

In preparation for the conference, in the cubbyholes of public buildings in the national capitals, zealous civil servants had prepared brave plans for the United Nations to be. One U.N. agency would eradicate the killer diseases, such as smallpox, and would open eyes closed by glaucoma. Another would erase illiteracy and spread understanding. Another extend technical assistance to backward regions. International trading of commodities basic to national economies (grains, oil, sugar, coffee) would be conducted at prices fair to producers and consumers. And the armies would cower before the might of the United Nations, assisted by a World Police Force. Too good those plans were, as it turned out, for the "have" states and the states bent on aggrandizement; and too good for statesmen insufficiently fired by the idealism of their people. And yet, too good also were those plans to be abandoned now!

On May 4, 1945, I woke up in sunny, pastel San Francisco to read black headlines. "16 Polish Leaders Arrested." They had left Warsaw on March 28 to meet with the Russian Army Command—under safe conduct. There were to have been discussions about the "free and unfettered elections" promised Poland at Yalta. Nothing was heard from the Polish leaders, in spite of diplomatic inquiries, until their arrests were announced by Soviet Foreign Minister Molotov in San Francisco. They had been guilty, he charged, of acts of sabotage in the rear of the Soviet armies marching on Berlin. In fact, the Soviets had begun the absorption of the Polish people into their empire. Stalin, like the fox who swallowed the rabbit, declared that Polish affairs were now an internal matter, and he refused to discuss them. After interrogation and months of solitary confinement the Polish leaders pleaded guilty in return for sentences of a year or two. A small foretaste of the fate of thousands of Poles who would be arrested and never heard of again. With the arrests, the U.N. Conference shuddered and almost broke up, as if a guest at a party had suddenly turned ugly, with loud, menacing threats.

Before I left San Francisco the ebb had begun from the dream of international order. States refused to cede any of their sovereignty. Plans for a U.N. Police Force were quickly discarded. Proposals that all should come to the aid of any victim of aggression were thwarted by the Big Power veto. Commodity trading was shuffled off to the tender mercies of the trans-national corporations; international loans and exchange rates to the bankers. Not that all has been lost. Some of the U.N. agencies have done good work; smallpox has been eradicated and literacy has been increased. Some of those agencies, however, UNESCO, for example, have become mired in boon-doggling, back-scratching and divisive polemics.

It's a little hard to keep the faith, Legs, and not cry, when you read the words of Article 26 of the Charter the nations approved in San Francisco 40 years ago. That Article pledges the founding members "to promote peace with the least diversion for armaments from the world's human and economic resources." Governments today, Canada included, hawk military wares on a scale that makes the Merchants of Death of bygone days seem like neighbourhood peddlers. Welcome aboard the good ship Armageddon! Twenty-five million men and women are enrolled in regular armed forces duty. More than a billion dollars a day is being spent on weapons while 40,000 daily die of malnutrition, that number going up instead of down. While the world focuses on nuclear stockpiles, the arsenal of conventional (!) weapons increases daily, in numbers and deadliness, out of the spotlight. Silicon chips are scanned for defects in order to bring pinpoint precision to missile deliveries. Star Wars are next, bespoken for by Ronald Reagan, who has already played a starring role in World War II (The Movie), Cold Wars I and II, and now Better Dead than Red (The Remake).

The gap between countries with more than enough and those with too little yawns wider, as it does between the well-off and the poor within nations. We'll have to content ourselves, Legs, with incremental steps toward unfurling the battle flags and inaugurating a Parliament of Man with restricted powers over key matters that affect every earthling. Atmospheric pollution, for example, is trans-national. Can you imagine a sapient World Court with power to enforce a Charter of elementary human rights? Are you frightened by visions of a Dr. No presiding over an evil empire? I think humans, of all skins, can run a decent council for the global village.

Of course there are admission prices to pay to a world of comity. Canada will have to surrender, not any of its prized virtue, but some of its autonomy. Shoot, just what autonomy would we lose? International finance is already beyond local control and who needs to keep a standing army just because another country needs to keep a standing army? We'll lose some social standing, and there'll be a levelling of incomes worldwide. So what? Set that beside the horrendous dangers of today, and anyway, the good green earth can succor all who crawl on its bosom if the politics are right.

I'll march in Vancouver in April with the annual peace rally, although street demonstrations haven't as much influence as they should have in the corridors of power. And I'll have to tuck in my feelings on one point as I march. I don't like to see our mortal friends, the Old Communists, grab top billing in those parades—just don't like any hidden private agendas or any Party that dares not speak its name.

This extinct volcano has finished its fulminating. Our policies have gotta have bottom, Legs! Who will provide long-term directions and depth if we don't? Even an iceberg doesn't dazzle for long if its bottom is flawed! If only we can do it without being pious! I can't, not that part anyway.

Epistolarily yours,

Alex

HOW CAN WE ANSWER
THE THUNDER ON THE RIGHT
WITHOUT LIGHTNING OF OUR OWN
ON THE LEFT?

En route by train
Stockholm to Paris
November 15, 1984

Dear Legs,

You were in fine fettle talking about the election in the locker room after our game. Was it because for once you thumped me? Not next time you won't! Enfeebled by age I'm not! There's nothing wrong with competition, Legs, though if by some miracle you persist in beating me, I'll have to rethink that one. Anyway I caught your every word—your matter and impertinency mixed—while I stood there, breathless and faint and leaning on my sword.

"Operation Survival!" That's what you called the NDP's campaign. Sure, most of our MPs survived. A little boy once asked his father, "What did you do in the Revolution, Daddy?" Daddy replied, "J'ai survive." Our survivors could say the same thing.

Prime Minister John Turner called the election to see if his polls were right. They weren't! Thank goodness it's over, though my election stints were pleasant enough. You did yours in a phone bank calling NDP voters to make sure they weren't getting any funny ideas. Meanwhile I was out a-walking some streets with Ian Waddell, playing the Squire of Vancouver East. Occasionally I even permitted myself to smile, although that is frowned upon in some circles.

Certainly the NDP didn't strain any brains in that election. Now its ship is safely back in calmer waters, with much the same crew, having weathered the storm, but light, Legs, awfully light, in the way of cargo in its hold.

What bothers me is that the NDP went along with the existing economic order in that campaign. No, we didn't accept all its warts; I'm not saying that. I am saying that the NDP failed to challenge the underlying assumptions of an economic system that is sharpening inequalities and producing an intolerable level of unemployment. How can we answer the thunder on the Right without some lightning of our own on the Left? I've already made that point? I have? Well it's worth making twice.

Yet for all that, it's better that you are more upbeat about our campaign than I am. I'm the spirit of elections past and you of those to come. Without faith and hope you can't help to set us on course. And were you ever talking good! Why, you said, if our Ed hadn't beaten the other two in the TV debate we'd have lost half our seats. He bested Brian, whose views are as spacious as his smile, and John, whose clothes are as old as his views. And what good, you exclaimed, standing starkers, are all my fine ideas without a strong NDP to work within to make them happen? And, you went on, hadn't it been a brilliant tactic to latch onto the polls that have the NDP identified as fighting for the little person and translate that into a concern for "ordinary Canadians." Was it Gerry Caplan, our National Secretary, who hit on that tactic? Gerry knows about the bad old times when the CCF had to turn stones over to find a left-thinking voter. He has a story about the New Brunswick election in 1944 when two CCF ballots turned up in one poll. "Some bastard," expleted the Returning Officer, "has voted twice!" Yet brilliant tactic notwithstanding, you, and I, and Gerry, know perfectly well that the NDP needs a long-term strategy as well as emergency tactics.

Our electioneering has to be compounded of perspiration, inspiration, entertainment and education. Please, never again, a campaign as contentless (or as dull) as that one! Yes, I heard you say that the NDP forced Brian and John to discuss its issues. To that you could add, "Eureka!" The NDP discovered that there is more than one sex. Moving right along! But the NDP didn't give, in billions, the tab of bringing women's earnings up to men's for comparable work without bringing the men's under some restraint. And it certainly didn't let a tabby cat out of the bag by confiding that fair pay for equal worth is impossible without a planned program of income redistribution. And, yes, the NDP did go after the rich tax dodger and maintained that the greedy fellow should pay at least 20 per cent in income tax. Stick it to them! That's almost half of what I pay now. And the NDP argued that government "largesse" to business should be used for what it is given for, which is plain enough, and worth saying. But, dammit, Legs, we're still into telling a fable from the 50s to serve as our economics. You know how it goes: government should cut taxes and spend more so that consumer demand rises and people are hired and pay more taxes to bring down the deficit—all, of course, without inflation or high interest rates. That won't work. Ordinary Canadians, like me, know it won't work. Too many of them have stopped taking us seriously. They send some of us to Parliament Hill only to keep an eye on the others.

What are we up to? Are we trying to sneak up on the Old Parties without being noticed? King Lear thought that was a capital idea. He vented his opinion on the blasted heath that "it were an excellent stratagem to shoe a troop of horse with felt" and, having "stolen" upon the enemy, "kill, kill, kill!" The trouble is that Lear was half mad when he said that. Midway in the campaign I see a headline where our Ed is reported as saying that the NDP has lost its stigma, meaning we're no longer seen as supporting Big Government and things of that ilk. Well I think I know where our stigma is and am willing to help him find it.

It's not for us to campaign on just ameliorating the lot of people in the existing market system. Nor to be content with more government spending, which, without lids, over-heats that system and sooner or later scorches the wrong people. We should always be for steps to be taken, few and short as they sometimes need be, that demonstrably lead toward a democratic socialist society. Steps and ends—these should be the subject matter of a Great Debate in our ranks, the sooner had the better. I'd rather the members of Vancouver East go into that debate than into discussing the purchase of a business computer in which to store the predilections of ten or twenty thousand voters who lean our way. Everything but their sexual orientation! And why not that too? Wouldn't Archie Bunker love to hear that he was in our "computer data-base"? "EE-DIT," he'd holler!

That debate should include discussion of your concern that some large publicly owned companies are giving socialism a bad name. You pick out B.C. Hydro, which has indeed become over-fat and blundersome of late. It has escaped from its keepers and brought on stream more electricity than the people who own it can conceivably use for years to come. As you say, that puts us into extra debt, in the billions, and, to make matters worse, the debt is repayable in American dollars that are 25 per cent costlier than when the loans were taken out, and rising all the time. (Did you forget that one of Hydro's loans is repayable in Canadian funds, it having been negotiated between a Jewish Premier and an Arab state?) Now Hydro is trying to peddle its surplus energy in California for whatever it can get. What can I say? Not that power exported at a half-decent price is bad; it's surely better to export ever-flowing water power than to deplete natural gas or even timber. But Hydro ought to have had the contract in hand before the river was dammed. It's blunders like that that led one voter to tell me that socialists couldn't, with any marked success, run a peanut stand. What cheek! (It's interesting that we get the blame when a Socred-run public corporation fails and the Socreds reap the praise when the private sector is doing well—though I can't recall the last time that happened.) I'll never agree that public ownership is more likely to result in poor performance than private ownership. In each it's a matter of deploying the best management techniques, even if feelings are hurt.

I found another part of the answer to your concern after travelling to Prince Rupert to deliver an Address. The Party sent me thither to hold the hands of the faithful after our MLA for the area, Graham Lea, had jumped the NDP ship. He thought himself inside out by dwelling too much on my sort of ideas. After unbottling another idea or two in my Address I sat in the hall with the technical manager of Prince Rupert's local telephone company. He was proud of his municipally owned system (the only one left in B.C.), which netted the city half a million dollars a year. Small can be Beautiful! That fellow changed my mind, and (cross your fingers) my new mind may work better. Why shouldn't large public enterprises be broken down into smaller units, publicly or co-operatively owned, which would compete with each other in service and efficiency?

There's more to the answer. Legislative Committees should oversee Crown Corporations to make sure they're not just protecting or fattening their own backsides. Bill Bennett set up such a watchdog committee in 1977, with me as one sapient member. It held hearings at which expert advice and research findings were submitted to assist us in formulating our recommendations. Alas, the silly fellow dissolved the Committee four years later in the name of restraint.

Canada has some well-run Crown Corporations whose purpose is not just to get by but also to serve the larger public good. Air Canada is one. That purpose is not shared by, as an example, non-Crown Corporations like the giant timber companies of this province. They cut and run from our forests with too much boodle and too little replanting. They still clear-cut three acres for every one that is properly restocked. And they get less wood from the log than the European countries, while manufacturing almost none of the wood into finished timber products. That, my dear fellow, is inefficiency on a grand and private scale.

We can't find enough jobs without a manufacturing base. But look at what just happened in Nanaimo. A U.S. company, AMCA International, proposed to set up shop to fabricate modules for the oil and gas industry. It claimed 700 people would be hired on. You and the labour movement said no, even though labour's opposition cost our Nanaimo MP the votes he needed to be re-elected. AMCA, you say, wanted too much: an industrial site from the government; training of its workers at Douglas College; and, the big one, a three-year union agreement with pay and benefits substantially below regular union rates. Further, the company wouldn't bid for the work without knowing the labour costs in advance. It insisted on a binding agreement before any workers appeared on the job to accept or reject its terms. Must we put with this, you ask, to get international business? Must we subsidize our coal exports to Japan on a handsome scale and also mark down the price of our labour for cheap export. I don't like—you've gathered that—two-tier labour rates, regular for shop work in Vancouver and sub-standard in Nanaimo. Well, overall, I can't disagree with you on this one.

And yet, Legs, there's a lean and hungry world off our shores. Modules? Bread! We don't even bake all of our bread anymore. Heavy bread is trucked in from

California. Shall we close up the casements, shut out the world, manufacture our own poverty in B.C.? What we need is realistic planning, including competitive labour costs. Why not manufacture our own manufacturing industry in B.C. to compete with AMCA? It'd make U.S. giants humbler in their demands. With a hard-headed NDP program for secondary industry, Ted Miller could have parried the local hysteria and won re-election.

What's that? I am out of my depth? I am? Do you realize that your disagreements have driven me, quite in the line of duty, to a northern land where the midnight sun made it hard for me to keep my virtue? And do you realize the indignities I suffered en route? In the City of Paris I was the victim of a robbery attempt by three kerchiefed Gypsy women who took social equality more seriously than I had bargained for. They swarmed upon me in a crowded Metro train, making loud kissing noises (the women, not the train), pretending to be deaf and dumb. One held a doll, swaddled like a baby, to catch my eye I suppose and as I groped for the feminine plural of "thief," they groped not for my jewels, but my wallet. "Voleuse," I cried, which aroused a little Frenchman to tug considerately at my sleeve in order to help me with my grammar. By now, Gypsy fingers roamed all over me. Leaving my wife, Dorothy, with a French Count in a castle on the River Loire, I pressed on manfully (sic) by train to Stockholm. When night fell the six in my compartment slept mutually in "couchettes" let down from the ceiling, with a pillow and blanket supplied by the porter.

In Copenhagen I made another way-stop for a walk in the Tivoli Gardens with a Tuborg. Elsewhere in that city I noticed that Porn had fallen on hard times. The sex shops were forlorn of customers, who had apparently supped full of titillation. The saturnine Danes maintain that sex crimes have also declined. Prudery is Pornography's Friend, Censorship its Banker.

I might have been in northern Ontario crossing Sweden

to Stockholm. Sweden is much like Canada in the raw splendor of its scenery and resources and is equally dependent upon international trade. It's a canard, by the way, started by Eisenhower, that suicide is more common in Sweden than in countries like Canada. I felt no urge to jump off a bridge while I was there. In fact, I took my own soundings with the word always coming back, "soldier on, Alex."

Things are seldom what they seem. The Swedish unions seem to be conservative as they hardly ever hit the bricks. In fact, they make the weather in their own country to a greater degree than trade unions do anywhere else. Swedish socialists are like businessmen at a Rotary lunch with their talk about "expanding the productive sector" and "the profitability of the export industries." Actually, they simply face the necessity of wealth creation in priority to its distribution. And those socialists take their time; oh, how they take their time! And yet the Swedish tortoise is still ahead of anyone else's hare in the realization of tangible socialist goals.

I didn't see Olof Palme, the Social Democratic Prime Minister, who has twice visited B.C. He was in Gotland at an "in" resort with his clothes off. Nor was Finance Minister Feldt (also a B.C. visitor) in town. He's known as the Boxer after being felled by a professional during a brawl in a hotel in Lulea. Only after hours, with some schnapps, does living become a laughing matter in a Swedish mouth. I did have an interview with Per-Olof Edin, who is called "the Expert in the Ministry of Finance," and who is the architect of the new Wage Earner Funds. Per was perfectly willing to answer my questions although not particularly interested in plumbing my own well of knowledge.

I met Per in the central union building and will paraphrase his answers as his English was too advanced for me.

"You know what they say about Sweden, Per, in the best clubs? They say Sweden is a Fools' Paradise with the wild welfare spending leading to large deficits and a poor trade balance."

"Do only Fools," he replied, "insist upon social safety net programs that prevent even the poorest and weakest from falling into poverty? Of course, social security depends upon a healthy, growing commodity economy and good export sales. And such growth does not come easily. Sweden is a small country that imports all of its oil and is highly sensitive to the world market and currency fluctuations. Still our Prime Minister rejects what he calls the 'social disarmament' of our welfare measures."

"I met a Swede with a cigar at the central station, Per, who thinks your spending is wild. He pointed to a government billboard urging couples to apply for a loan for their dream house. It was bad enough, he said, for the government to encourage cohabitation without asking couples to come and get his tax payments. Was he a fool?"

"Oh," said Per, "if he had been a carpenter, like his Maker, he'd have been glad enough of the work to build a home."

"Your taxes are high. You'd have even lost Ingmar Bergman, your moody movie maker, to a sunny tax haven if the Prime Minister himself hadn't pleaded with him."

"Yes, our taxes are high, with no special loopholes for the well-to-do." (Per looked sad when he said that, so I threw in the words of Thomas Aquinas from the fourteenth century about taxes being simply "to provide for the common good from the common goods." Straight off he was his old self.)

"I understand, Per, that Wage Earner Funds, initiated by the labour movement, were a tough issue for the Social Democrats in the election in 1982. Businessmen said they would make the unions too strong and even some unions were opposed to the Funds, saying they were a poor substitute for larger pay increases."

"Yes, and after the election 75,000 Swedes marched in a protest demonstration. Now the Funds have been established in law and the government hopes to rally more support behind them. There will be five Regional Funds administered by Boards appointed by the government, with majority worker representation. The Funds will be allotted investment capital through a combination of profit sharing and payroll deductions, a 20 per cent levy on profits over a certain level, and a 0.2 per cent levy on wages. They will also administer some Pension Reserves. The Funds will purchase shares in industry and advance venture capital to promising new companies. Their investments must return at least 3 per cent in real terms."

"What led the Social Democrats and labour to adopt this program?"

"First we took into account the lopsided distribution in wealth and power. Of all Swedish households, 89 per cent own no shares at all. Social equality cannot come through welfare and tax policies alone or even income policies. Property ownership must be widely diffused.

"Secondly, we recognize that laws for Co-Determination, including worker representation on Corporate Boards and profit sharing, only go so far toward industrial democracy. Profit sharing may give workers shares in the company they work for, but the chances are they will be sold and fall back to the original owners. Collective capital formation is also necessary.

"In the third place we wish to extend and improve our policies of Wage Solidarity. Sweden has come a long way toward equal wages for similar work through central bargaining between unions and the employers' association. We have also reduced the spread between higher and lower paid workers by almost half in the fifteen years before the defeat of the Social Democrats in 1976. However, fair wage averaging results in excessive profits in stronger companies that would otherwise pay higher wages. The Funds will draw on these excess profits.

"Fourthly—the most compelling reason—the industrial sector is too small. Enduring growth presupposes a steady stream of venture capital, national in origin. The Funds will add to private investment as well as give workers some responsibility for investment decisions."

"I am thinking of Canada, Per. We too have a shrinking productive base."

"That is true," said Per, "of all the western economies. Sweden, however, rejects the so-called free enterprise solution to the common problem. Reaganism seeks to spur growth by using high profits and low wages to transfer funds from the wage earning to the industrial side. To do this means to weaken or destroy unions. That approach uses unemployment to keep price increases down. There is a crass indifference to how wealth is shared. Sweden will not pay the costs of Reaganism, which are calculated in human misery and social injustice. Our solution is fundamentally different."

"Ah, but is not Reagan surging toward re-election on a growth in incomes and employment and lower inflation?"

"Yes, with the pump primed by an annual deficit of $200 billion, a jobless rate never under 7 per cent and an unfavourable trade balance in goods and services of $100 billion a year. There will be corrections."

"Well, I must say, Per, your fundamentally different solution is a tall order. You give workers shares they can't cash or trade; you give them to all workers even if they don't work for a company that contributes to the Funds. You ask the Swedish people to put off having jam today for more jam tomorrow. How can you get them to take your order?"

"Not easily. Remember, though, that 90 per cent of Swedish workers, full- and part-time, male and female, are union members. Our unions have a strong ideological commitment to full employment and social equality. They also support high productivity and competitive prices that allow us to do business in the international markets. They know that full employment and social justice depend upon an orderly, limited growth in earnings.''

"Trade union friends in Canada say that they won't give up bargaining for as much as they can get until they know what a new system will give them in return.''

"Neither will our unions. They have always used their strength as bargaining chips to get things that benefit all working people—such as social programs, job creation in the public sector, taxation without special favours, day-care for working parents. They support the Funds as instruments to make gains in real wages all round.''

"And to make for full employment?''

"Only alongside our other policies. Eleven per cent of our budget goes to Manpower policies, chiefly government-sponsored job creation and training. Idleness destroys the individual's feeling of self-esteem and community, and increases criminality and alcoholism. Our calculations show that the cost of paying average wages to employ people to meet social needs is only slightly higher than paying them unemployment compensation, when losses in tax revenues and social security contributions are taken into account. We also shorten work time to spread it further, through parental leaves, Sabbaticals, flexible retirement rules, paid training and education, strict limits on overtime. Sweden, however, still cannot afford to reduce the 40-hour work week. Everything depends upon a strong industrial base.''

Summer, the Swedes say, is sometimes on a Thursday. A light sheet rain fell as I walked to the Swedish Research Centre. There I fell into a lively discussion with a group of ardent, no-go-slow socialists. To bring them on I played the part of a rather staid, stuffy Canadian tourist (my God, myself?). "Why,'' I said, "you've got the Swedish people strolling down the garden path with those Funds. In time, working people will have the whole thing."

"Not quite," one replied, "we're strolling at a snail's pace. The Funds are for an experimental period and, presently anyway, can own only 8 per cent of any company."

"I can see," I said, "that you don't have the patience of the young St. Francis of Assisi. He ardently favoured chastity, but was content to let it come, later, later. You want it right now. Aren't the Social Democrats in the political fight of their lives just to get the Funds started?"

There was a moment's silence. As a comely secretary served coffee, I asked, not missing the irony, if they were not pleased at closing the gender gap in Sweden. "Are not eight out of ten Swedish women working, full- or part-time, at wages virtually comparable to men's?"

"True, but still only one-third of our day nursery needs have been met." And another added (looking suspiciously female) that there had not been sufficient sightings in Sweden of the New Man (with apron and dustbuster?).

"Yet," I went on, "you've got to be pleased that Sweden has evened incomes and raised average living standards more than any other country."

"We are pleased," said one, "but we still have our share of parasitic wheeler-dealers and rapacious individuals. The gospel of greed has spread abroad, like a rumour, infecting the sane social democracies of northern Europe." No rest for the Virtuous!

Yet for all that, they boast about how their country leads the world in those things that make up the good life. If social equality is one of those things, they boast rightfully.

An ideological debate rages among our Swedish friends, Legs. Is too much central economic planning incompatible with political and civil liberties? Are the eastern European countries testimony of that? The Swedish Government is pursuing a middle course. The Funds will grow only with public approval. They will be self-governing and disperse decision-making. They presuppose and will invigorate the best features of the market system—risk-taking ventures of the public, private and co-operative type. Consumer choice will dictate needs. Social Welfare systems are assured! That middle course is the cutting edge of political and economic democracy.

Peripatetically yours,

Alex

IT'S LATER THAN WE THINK, LEGS

The Legislature
Victoria, B.C.
March 5, 1985

My dear Legs,
   I returned from Sweden a wiser and a wider man. Wiser
from meeting people even slightly smarter than I am and
wider from run-ins with Swedish meat balls you have since
run off me. Brace yourself for one last short letter and
that'll be it. Frankly, I've mined myself out, and I refuse
to mine my slag heaps. Someday, who knows, in a year or
three, I may come up with more nuggets and by then
should have the hang of the electric pencil sharpener.
   I've closed the door of my little cubbyhole of an office.
The Opposition Caucus rooms spook me with Dave gone.
Fifteen years ago I worked as hard to elect Dave Barrett
our Provincial Leader as you worked last year to make
Bob Skelly his successor. Now I miss Dave's feisty,
ebullient leadership. Once, when we were government
Dave blew his top after Jack Radford, our Wildlife
Minister, kept asking for more money to shoot bears or
rapids or something. Dave leapt onto the Cabinet table in
stocking feet and rushed over to Jack. "No way," he said,
planting his terrycloth socks in front of Jack's pile of
arguments. At another Cabinet meeting, after every

Minister gave a different opinion, Dave delivered his own
and rounded it off with "now we have a consensus. All
opposed to my opinion signify by saying 'I resign.'" How
he'd like to be here these days tying into Bennett when that
benighted fellow stings the students and parents of B.C.
with yet more educational cut-backs, as if determined to
make pin-heads of us all.

I'd like to educate Canadians, while they are still
literate, to set up Investment Funds similar to those in
Sweden. It's later than we think, Legs. Last week the
Canadian dollar was down to 72 cents in its fall through
the international skies. Our national debt rises over the
Rideau River to an altitude where we will soon be
borrowing to pay the interest on past borrowing. The other
day my son-in-law, the policeman, told of seeing 400
perfectly good men and women in a food bank line on
Cordova Street. You bet we need limits to living too high
on the hog and seed capital to get more people working in
useful enterprises. B.C. residents, I'm told, have $36
billion socked away in savings. What's it doing?

Of course, Canadian Wage Earner Funds will have to
grow out of our own social realities. We have many
regions varying from one another and should have more
than five funds. They should also represent the general
public to a greater extent than the trade unions, given our
unions as they are today and the numbers they speak for.

I should have mentioned, by the way, in my last letter,
that Sweden has conscription and devotes no less than 10
per cent of its national budget to defence. Both are
accepted by Left and Right with little dissent. Defence
spending, by general agreement, is a necessity to make
Sweden's neutrality "credible." Sweden conscripts young
men (not women!) for nine months, sometimes more.
They receive training and are put through exercises and
manoeuvres under some measure of discipline, but not all
that much.

Canadians don't need military conscription in order to make peaceful co-existence more credible. We have to our south and north two weapons systems with over-kill to the Nth degree. If they collide we are squashed anyway. Enrolling young men *and* women in universal national service should not, however, be dismissed out of hand. A surer bridge between school and working life can strengthen a country and its people. There are any number of useful projects to get ahead with in towns and wilderness. Carrying them out, with the aid of a pinch of discipline, can instill a sense of pride and purpose in the years when those things matter most. Do you think I sound too stodgy? Well let me refer you to an old *New Yorker* cartoon. The old fellow sitting at the bar says to his young hippie companion: "Listen, kid, I hated America before you were born."

Needless to say, Swedish conscription applies evenly to well-off and poorer. Do you recall, Legs, that my Swedish friends insisted upon "social equality" as a prime ingredient in the recipe of what constitutes the good life? A spiritual not a material value. Imagine that! Some purblind reactionaries would have me believe that people lead the most satisfying lives when they live in a country with a high average per capita income. Idiots! I have a pretty good idea of your yardstick for measuring the good life. I listen to you when you think I am not (and I'd be grateful if you'd return the favour). Clean air and rivers, a satisfying work experience, health and life expectancy, travel, access to education and the arts, lots of affection, your list goes on. You also taught me to appreciate "small socialism." You said you walked east on Hastings Street passing run-down buildings, people staggering out of beer parlours, the police keeping an eye on them, until you came to the old Carnegie Library at Main Street. Thanks to local activists, and Mayor Harcourt, that disused library is now a community centre. Inside you saw a Native Indian family playing basketball in the gym, a reading room spread with papers and magazines, a small movie theatre. There was not only central heating, but, in the air, companionship and an aura of individual self-esteem. Community centres, you know, could be used for community administration as well as recreation. Citizen groups could get together in them to help police in local crime control, act as advice givers, even take over some of what we call social assistance.

You also have a quality that I found in my Swedish friends, a determination not to accept unemployment and an impoverished under-class. What's so great about that? Don't all NDPers, including myself, share that resolve? Yes, in a way, but how many of us really have the will (I think you're one of them) to carry the burdens and confront the difficulties of getting rid of unemployment and poverty? "Vice," wrote Alexander Pope, is a monster which

> *Seen too oft, familiar with her face*
> *We first endure, then pity, then embrace.*

We're seduced by what we haven't the guts to change and learn to call it human nature, the natural order of things, God's will . . .

If the Swedes are ahead of us it's because, through long socialist education, they have a greater respect for others and the next generation. That's indispensable to social and economic progress. Our plans must go ahead with popular support. The problems are political, not economic. And the solutions require a revolution in basic contemporary values. I used to think that all we had to do was win power and change the economic institutions. So did the poet Stephen Spender, when he too was much younger. He imagined himself looking backward and wondering how it had been

That Works, Interest, Building, Money
Could ever hide
The palpable and obvious love of man for man

Ah, but do the Works promote individual selfishness or does selfishness create the Works? In fact one augments the other in a fine interaction. Spender and I were naive, though that's not a bad thing. Naivite may be the mother of invention! Woodsworth was right in equating the political and economic struggle with the need for a new set of values. Our attack has to be two-pronged, Legs, political programs and socialist education.

With time out, of course, for our regular game of squash.

Yours for my Sabbatical,

Alex